The Manager's Pocket Guide to
Virtual Teams

Richard Bellingham, Ed.D.

HRD Press, Inc. • Amherst • Massachusetts

Published by:

HRD Press
22 Amherst Road
Amherst, MA 01002
1-800-822-2801 (U.S. and Canada)
413-253-3488
413-253-3490 (FAX)
www.hrdpress.com

ISBN 0-87425-615-1

Cover design by Donna Thibault-Wong
Editorial services by Sally M. Farnham
Production services by Anctil Virtual Office

Printed in Canada

Introduction and Overview
Using Teams and Technology to Respond to Business Drivers

The Business Drivers

We hear about it on TV, read about it in newspapers and magazines and talk about it formally and informally. By now, most people are aware that massive changes are taking place in the business world. The industrial age continues to give way to the information and electronic age. The factors creating these changes include:

- **The global village**—Businesses are being forced to compete in a global economy where competition for quality goods at competitive prices is coming from all corners of the world. The emerging economies are placing competitive pressure on companies as never before. As trade barriers crumble, opportunities and challenges are created. The global village is also creating a more culturally diverse work force. Through this diversity comes creative opportunity as well as challenge.

- **Customer-focused relationships**—The consumer's increasing demand for better quality means companies that are flexible and able to respond quickly to market changes will remain competitive. Today, the new challenge is to develop interdependent relationships with customers to provide tailored solutions for their specific

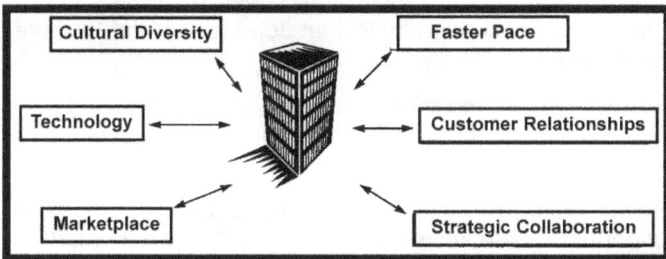

Cultural Diversity | Faster Pace

Technology | Customer Relationships

Marketplace | Strategic Collaboration

problems and opportunities. This shift in relationship (from "order taker" to "partner") has imposed enormous new demands on organizations. We can no longer be content when our customer satisfaction ratings are high; we have to respond, personalize and initiate solutions that result in customer growth.

- **Faster pace**—The increasing development and availability of electronic communications technology, such as fax, telephone, modem, satellite transmission, Internet communication and computer software, are creating a faster-paced workflow with greater flexibility and less dependence on the traditional office concept. Product development and redesign cycles have become increasingly compressed. "Faster" has become the corporate mantra. We are the fastest generation on record. Anything that makes things happen faster is readily adopted and admired. Speed has become a major competitive factor.

- **Strategic collaboration**—Companies who were once bitter adversaries are shifting attitudes to a more cooperative existence when combining their strengths builds a better mousetrap than either could build separately.

The Impact of Teaming

Organizations most likely to succeed during this storm of change are those willing to take a new look at the way they do business, particularly their work-force structure. Traditional hierarchical corporate structure is permanent, structured and rigid. A new, more effective model is the Fishnet Model created by Robert Johanson of the Institute for the Future.

The Fishnet organization is flexible—able to form and reform various patterns of relationship among managers and workers.

Events either external or internal that create challenges or opportunities are known as "spikes" in the Fishnet model.

Companies respond to the spikes by building teams of diverse workers to reach the organization's immediate goals, then dismantle the team to create new teams. The Fishnet model allows for fluid redefining of roles and leadership, while retaining its strength and interconnections.

This new model is gaining increasing acceptance because it is:

- Business driven rather than organizationally driven
- Dynamic and flexible
- Worldwide and cross-cultural
- Cross-functional
- Inter-enterprise

What Are Virtual Teams?

The challenges of teams today are different from those of the recent past. Today, many teams are geographically dispersed. They may also come from different disciplines, departments or even different organizations. We call this type of team a *Virtual Team*.

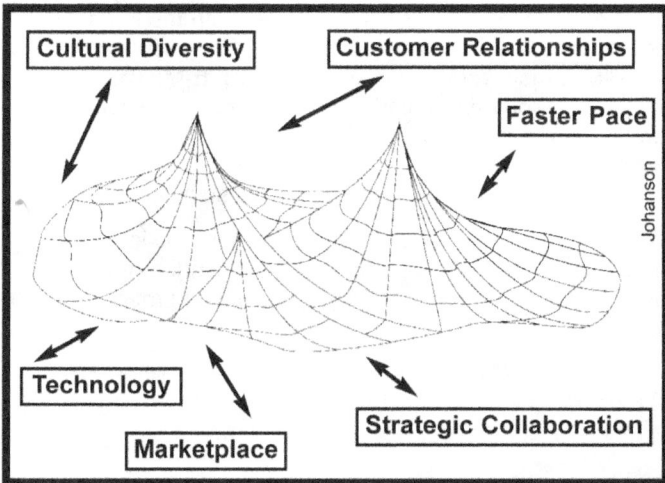

The advantage of virtual teams is that there are no geographic or organizational boundaries. By using modern communication technology, virtual teams can bring the best and brightest individuals together without the cost and trouble of travel or relocation.

Teams today need to develop trust and collaborate in a virtual world. But trust and collaboration are difficult when people are physically separated for long periods of time.

The essential elements of high performing teams need to be developed among people all over the world, who may not know each other and who may work together on a team only for a few months. Creating high performing teams, therefore, not only requires a solid foundation on the basics of teamwork, but also requires enabling technologies to accelerate and sustain progress.

The Role of Technology

Working without boundaries. Workgroup technology is a collection of computer software applications developed to allow individual team members to work together on projects regardless of geographic location. Workgroup technology generally works in tandem with the latest communication technologies, such as fax, modem, satellite transmission, laptop computers, E-Mail, etc. This technology particularly enhances communication and interpersonal group activity. It cannot perform the tasks of a project, but it enhances and supports the individuals working on a project from disparate locations.

Work anytime, anywhere. There are four basic time/space configurations for groups to work together using communications technology and workgroup technology.

• **Same Time/Same Place**—the traditional concept of meetings in which each member of the team comes together at a specific location and time.

- **Same Time/Different Place**—members meet together at the same time, but may be in different locations aided by technology such as telephone conference calling or video teleconferencing. Workgroup technology enhances this process by allowing more than one person to work on the same file at the same time from different locations.

- **Same Place/Different Time**—members work on the project within the same location but come and go at different times.

- **Different Time/Different Place**—members work on projects at different times and different locations using both workgroup and communication technology.

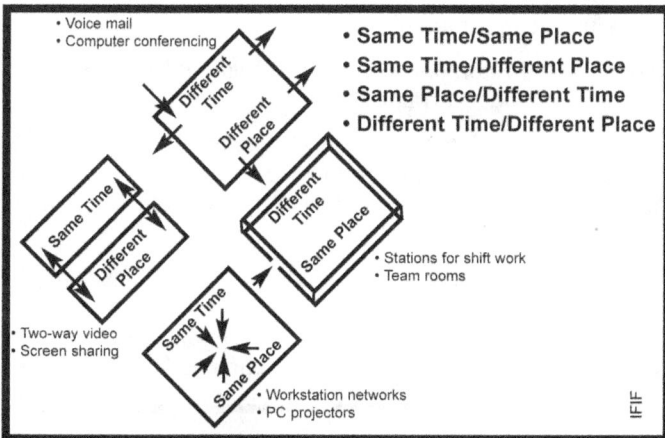

In the future the concept of any time/any place teamwork will increasingly provide flexibility and speed for bringing new products and services to the demanding marketplace at an ever increasing pace.

The new team technologies help virtual teams function, but a high performing team still requires strong team development skills to maximize the usefulness of the technology.

Additionally, the management of the communication continuum needs to be fluid and flexible. That is, knowing when to use a specific time/space configuration is key to managing team performance. Different points in the team process require different structures. The successful leader will be attuned to the needs of the team at each stage of development and adjust the communication model accordingly.

Team Technology Supports Collaboration

Workgroup technology is designed to promote collaboration. Working together in collaboration can be not only a rewarding experience, but has traditionally facilitated some of the greatest human creations.

Where would Elton John have been without lyricist Bernie Taupin? Or Rodgers without Hammerstein?

Although our society often rewards competition, it is through collaboration that many great scientific discoveries have been made. In fact, it has been said that competition chokes the creative process.

We define collaboration as two or more individuals with complementary skills working together to create a shared understanding that none had previously possessed or could have come to on their own (Schrage, 1990).

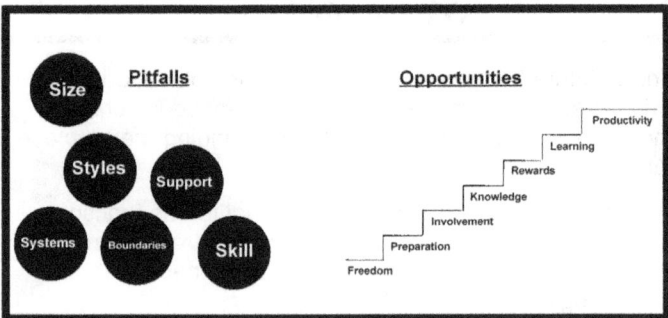

Organizations that support and reward collaboration will meet the emerging challenges of change, taking advantage of the global economy, new technology and cultural diversity to bring better quality products and services to ever demanding customers.

Implications for Organizational Dynamics

Pitfalls. Managers know that teams can be more effective than individuals working alone. Yet how do they know if their team will function at a high performance level? We have found there are several major pitfalls to developing and sustaining high performing teams. Before any work is done to develop a team, there are certain basic "pitfall" questions that need to be asked:

- Is this team the right size?
- Do team members have complementary skills and styles?
- Are there adequate systems for learning and communicating?
- Does the work environment support teamwork?
- Does the loss of boundaries in a virtual environment create new challenges?

Answering these questions will give you the foundation for building an effective team.

Opportunities. Just as there are potential pitfalls to developing a high performing team, there are also possibilities for leveraging the unique characteristics of a technology-enabled virtual team. If you are working in a virtual environment, keeping these opportunities in mind will heighten your team's performance:

- Preparing messages carefully before sending them
- Involving people in an electronic environment who may not be comfortable in groups
- Seeking the right person for an answer, even if you don't know who the right person is
- Rewarding desired behaviors and actual competence

- Documenting ideas
- Facilitating group learning
- Providing personal freedom through anywhere, anytime communications
- Creating virtual hand-offs around the globe that allows 24-hour work

In addition to leveraging these opportunities, we need to consider the organizational dynamics that yield high performance in traditional teams and find ways to apply those dynamics to virtual teams.

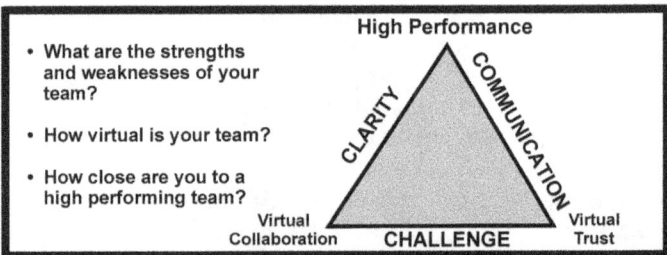

- **What are the strengths and weaknesses of your team?**
- **How virtual is your team?**
- **How close are you to a high performing team?**

High Performance / CLARITY / COMMUNICATION / Virtual Collaboration / CHALLENGE / Virtual Trust

TEAM ASSESSMENT

As a starting point for team development, it may be helpful to assess your team today. On the next few pages you will find three assessment tools. The first tool will help you measure how your team is functioning today. The second tool will measure the degree of virtuality required of the team. The third assessment will give you an idea of what stage of development your team is in today.

1 Team Effectiveness Profile

To get a sense of your team's strengths and weaknesses, complete the assessment instrument on the next page, using the table below for your ratings:

Score	Strength	Importance to the business	Direction
5.00	Strongly agree	Critical	Getting much better
4.00	Agree	Very important	Getting better
3.00	Somewhat agree	Important	About the same
2.00	Disagree	Somewhat important	Getting worse
1.00	Strongly disagree	Not important	Getting much worse

1 Team Effectiveness Profile

You will know a group of people has evolved into a high performing team when there is uniformly high commitment, there is adequate capacity to do the job (e.g., skills and resources), and there is team culture in which accountability, personal development and success are highly valued. The Team Effectiveness Profile summarizes specific norms from the literature on team development into these three categories: commitment, capacity, and culture. Using the table on the previous page, write down the numeric score that best matches what is true for you for each of the three columns on each question.

	Strength	Importance	Direction
Commitment			
We have a shared vision of what's possible for our team.			
We have a common purpose.			
We have challenging performance goals.			
We have opportunities for personal development.			
We receive constructive feedback.			
We are rewarded fairly for our contributions.			
We are rewarded as a team.			
Roles and responsibilities are clear.			
The organization is concerned about our well being.			
Capacity			
We have the skills we need to meet our requirements.			
We have complementary skills.			
We have complementary styles.			
We have the resources and tools we need to meet our requirements.			
Team members demonstrate excellence in their work habits.			

(Team Assessment continues on next page.)

1 Team Effectiveness Profile *(concluded)*

Culture	Strength	Importance	Direction
We are accountable for our performance.			
There is a high level of trust in our team.			
We have open, honest, direct communications.			
People think interdependently on the team.			
We seek ways to support each other.			
We are involved in decisions that affect us.			
We strive to perform at the highest possible quality.			
We are innovative.			
We have fun.			
We are empowered to do our jobs.			
We encourage multiple perspectives when accomplishing tasks.			
Successes and failures are shared collectively.			
We respect each other.			
We function as a unit.			

(Team Assessment continues on next page.)

2 Virtuality Assessment

For each of the statements below, circle one number on the continuum scale that best represents your team's characteristics. The 1 represents the statement on the left and 5 represents the statement on the right.

My team has the following characteristics:

We're in the same physical work space.	1 2 3 4 5	We're in many workplace locations.
We're in the same time zone with the same work hours.	1 2 3 4 5	We're in many time zones with flexible work hours.
We're at the same level within the organization.	1 2 3 4 5	We're from many levels within the organization.
We're in the same department.	1 2 3 4 5	We're from many departments.
We're in the same organization.	1 2 3 4 5	We're from many organizations.
We live and work in the same culture.	1 2 3 4 5	We're from many diverse cultures.

(Team Assessment continues on next page.)

3 Stage of Development Assessment

Answer the following questions to get a snapshot assessment of the stage of development your team is functioning in right now. For each of the questions below, circle the number on the scale that best represents your team's characteristics.

Stage 1. Orientation

| We are unsure of why we are part of the group. | 1 2 3 4 5 | We feel a sense of belonging to the group. |

Stage 2. Trust Building

| We do not feel comfortable expressing our opinions. | 1 2 3 4 5 | We have revealed our true agenda for being part of the group. |

Stage 3. Goal Clarification

| We are struggling over conflicting objectives. | 1 2 3 4 5 | We understand what we're trying to accomplish. |

Stage 4. Decision Making

| Our roles conflict and overlap with one another. | 1 2 3 4 5 | We are clear about roles and tasks. We are now ready to focus on getting to work. |

Stage 5. Implementation

| We do not know the specific work that needs to be done. | 1 2 3 4 5 | It is clear who does what, when, and where, and we are productive. |

Stage 6. High Performance

| We are overwhelmed by the amount of work that needs to be done. | 1 2 3 4 5 | There is true synergy in the group. The group together is greater than the sum total of the individuals. |

Stage 7. Renewal

| We feel burned out, defeated and irritable. We are not interested in continuing. | 1 2 3 4 5 | We re-evaluate our vision and goals at the end of each major task. We build back lessons learned into how we do our work. |

Task I.
Challenge Performance

Key Ingredients:
- Stretch objectives
- Balanced needs

Critical Skills:
1. Prioritize major issues and opportunities
2. Develop a common purpose

Introduction

We define a team as two or more individuals who are working together toward a common goal and/or a meaningful purpose. The four parts that define a team are:

1. **Common goal**—Although each team member has a clear individual responsibility, each member shares in the commitment of achieving a common goal.

2. **Team identity**—Each member sees themselves as a member of the group as a whole.

3. **Interdependence**—The goals could not be accomplished by the efforts of a single team member; each member is dependent on the other members.

4. **Common set of norms**—The group members establish an agreed upon set of values, behaviors and rules that govern the group.

High Performance Teams

Assigning a group of people to a team does not in itself yield the benefits of teamwork as we described. The wide variability in team performance is due to how well individuals work together and the clarity of the objectives the group is trying to achieve. High performing teams:

- Clearly understand and are committed to a common goal
- Are creative, innovative and flexible
- Share an enthusiasm for working together
- Find that the group energy adds to the individual energy
- Are results-oriented
- Have clearly defined roles with good, clear communication
- Recognize the diversity and individual strengths of its members and utilize them to a positive advantage
- Are supportive of one another
- Deal with conflict through open communication based on mutual trust and respect
- Share leadership
- Evaluate the team performance to refine and make changes as needed

The *V*irtual Challenge

When modern teams form in a virtual setting, it is important to understand that each team member has a different perspective. At the same time, we must establish a common agreement of what defines high performance. Therefore, to challenge performance, we must be sensitive to individual, organizational and cultural perspectives.

**Team Technology Meets the Needs of Each Stage
in Team Development**

During a single project any or all four of the workgroup technology options may be used to maximize the effectiveness and productivity of the team. Most teams move through a common set of phases during the course of their work together (Gibb and Young). Each phase must be processed before the group can move onto the next phase. The workgroup technology options (time/place) can enhance and support each phase.

1. **Orientation**—Often in this initial stage of new team development, face-to-face contact helps establish relationships. In this phase, the team gains a sense of its purpose and why it has been brought together. Members should develop a sense of belonging. Same Time/Same Place technology (e.g., PC projectors) can enhance this stage of the project.

2. **Building trust**—Trust is an important part of any successful team, but especially in a virtual environment when face-to-face contact is minimal. During this phase, it is important for stated and hidden agendas to be openly revealed. As with the orientation stage, same time/same place meetings will enhance the trust-building process. If this is not possible, then communication enhanced by workgroup technology can help build trust and familiarity among team members. In the trust-building phase team members have a need to get to know each other and get a sense of who they are working with. Building team profiles into your use of workgroup technology can greatly aid in this "who are you" phase.

3. **Defining goals and roles**—In this phase team members develop a common purpose and define what each person must do and how they will do it. During this stage team members need to feel their ideas are recognized and understood, and they often need immediate feedback. Same time/ different place technology (e.g., brainstorming and

consensus-building technology) can enhance the process by allowing all members of the team to communicate at the same time regardless of location.

4. **Decision making**—Once the group has decided where it is going by defining its goals, it is time to determine "how are we going to get there." The group identifies tasks to be done, who should do them and any conflicts and interdependencies. A schedule is created with major milestones indicated for how the group will reach its goal. The group becomes ready to get working.

5. **Implementation**—This is where the group rolls up its sleeves and gets to work. Often time pressure becomes crucial and team members are too busy to assemble at a particular time. Now that roles and norms have been established different time/different place workgroup technologies (e.g., voice mail, computer conferencing, electronic database) enhance the flexibility and speed of this stage, allowing team members to work on their own time schedule and location while maintaining communication with others.

6. **High performance**—The team breaks through into a high level of functioning in which each team is intuitively able to respond to changing conditions and uses the features of team technology to enhance performance.

   As in the implementation stage, the different time/different place and same place/different time models are used the most at this stage.

7. **Closure or renewal**—At the end of the project or phase of a project, the team has a need to again come together in a same time/same place option. Face-to-face communication facilitates the need to celebrate or grieve depending on the results of the project. It also enables the group through the evaluation process, learning process and recharging for the next phase of a project.

Team Motivation

Teams function at their highest levels when they have "stretch" objectives. Stretch objectives provide a level of challenge so that each team member is motivated to push the envelope beyond their previous achievements.

Stretch objectives must be seen as reachable for the team to pull together to make them happen. Unreachable goals discourage, rather than encourage.

Finding the right balance between stretching the team's abilities and making the goals achievable is an essential element of team success.

Teams tend to flourish when their leaders focus on performance results that balance a wide scope of needs including customers, employees, suppliers, and shareholders. Results that only focus on financial performance do not have the same motivating effect as results that serve a greater purpose.

In this section your task will be to challenge performance. To accomplish this, you will learn two skills:

Skill 1. Prioritize major issues and opportunities

Skill 2. Develop a common purpose

Customer Satisfaction   Employees
Share-Holder Returns   Suppliers
Financial Performance   Community

SKILL 1:
PRIORITIZE MAJOR ISSUES
AND OPPORTUNITIES

- **Definition:** Generates intellectual and emotional excitement through compelling challenges and exciting opportunities
- **Benefits:**
  - Creates common ground, ésprit de corp
  - Reflects the aspirations of the team
- **Steps:**
  - A. Identify changes and challenges
  - B. Identify make-or-break issues
  - C. Problem solve top priorities

Introduction

Prioritizing major issues and opportunities is a way to generate intellectual and emotional excitement in your team. By reviewing and analyzing the factors affecting the internal and external environment, your team lays the foundation for creating a common vision and purpose for the task at hand. This analysis should lead to identification of the "Fishnet spikes" around which the organization needs to mobilize. Evaluating changes and challenges, identifying key issues and setting top priorities are the three steps that lead to motivating the team through a compelling challenge or exciting opportunity. This excitement creates a sense of unity and provides a reason for working together.

The three steps to prioritizing major issues and opportunities:

Step A. Identify changes and challenges.
Step B. Identify make or break issues.
Step C. Problem solve top priorities.

The Virtual Challenge

During these initial stages, it is especially important for team members to have equal access to all background information needed to prioritize the major issues. Members must be allowed to contribute to the process. Leaders need to create a forum for members to submit their ideas and should encourage full participation from all members. Discussion databases, voting software and ranking software can enhance this process.

Step A.
Identify changes and challenges

- **What it means:**
  - Understanding the internal and external conditions that may affect the business
- **How it works:**
  - Identify the changes occurring in the environment
  - Identify threats and opportunities
  - Identify challenges

The Idea

In the introduction, we discussed key business drivers that impact teams and impose new demands for technology and rapid response. Within the context of these broad marketplace changes, it is important to understand the specific changes affecting your business.

Changes and challenges come from multiple sources. Externally, there may be changes in:

- Customer demands,
- Marketplace conditions,
- Technology,
- Socio-demographic trends, or
- The state of the economy.

Searching the Internet is an effective way to gather information for your external scan.

Internally, there may be changes in:

- Leadership,
- Sales trends,
- Financial results,
- Employee opinions,
- Product development, or
- Operations.

All of these changes may create challenges or opportunities for your team.

Example

The IBToys Company is a new collaborative venture between a computer manufacturer and a toy company to develop and market a computer targeted specifically to children. A team of engineers, software designers, toy builders and marketing professionals from both companies have been brought together as a team to create this new product. As the team scans their external environment to understand the changes and challenges affecting their project, they discover several challenges as well as opportunities for this new venture.

Economy: Expanding, particularly for the market most likely to buy.

Customer: Parents increasing desire to provide toys that teach.

Technology: Voice activated commands and multi-media, interactive technology well suited to child-friendly computers.

Marketplace: Tremendous competition in the computer and software market. Falling prices, lower margins.

Social: Backlash from the 1980's, people want the simpler ways of life.

Political: Cuts in education could reduce numbers of computers in the classrooms.

The Virtual Challenge

One of the challenges in a virtual team environment is that there may be multiple environments to scan both externally and internally, particularly with teams from different organizations or different cultures. The team may need to narrow or define the boundaries and scope of the project and what the scan should include.

In multi-organizational teams, if trust has not been established, team members may withhold sensitive or competitive information gained from the internal and external scans.

YOUR TURN

Use the chart below to conduct an external and internal scan of changes that may affect your organization or team:

External Condition	Change that Occurred	Challenge it Represents
Economy		
Customer		
Technology		
Marketplace		
Social		
Political		

Internal Condition	Change that Occurred	Challenge it Represents
Leadership		
Marketing/sales		
Human resources		
Financial results		
Legal issues		
Information services		
Product development		
Operations/manufacture		

Continue this exercise by answering the questions on the following page.

YOUR TURN

Reviewing the Charts you wrote on the previous page, what appears to you to create the biggest "spikes" in your organization?

How does this "spike" impact your organization?

Who do you need to mobilize to make this happen? As you define participants in the team, think BIG—for example, think beyond the boundaries of your organization.

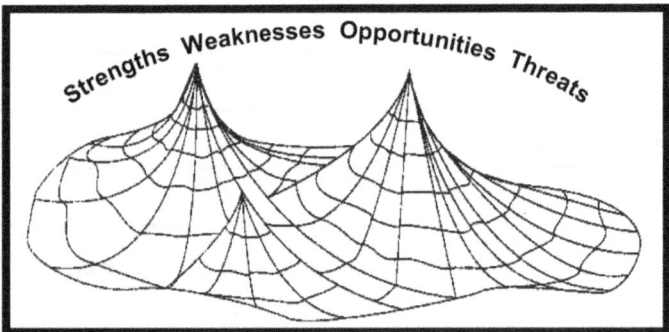

Strengths Weaknesses Opportunities Threats

Step B.
Identify make-or-break issues

- **What it means:**
  - — A comprehensive process for focusing on priorities
- **How it works:**
  - — Review internal and external challenges
  - — Understand team concerns
  - — Select the five more important:
    - practical
    - doable
    - high impact

The Idea

There are always more problems to solve than we have time to address. One key to team development is to have a set of priorities everyone agrees are critical to success. On most teams every member has a different image of the make or break issues—there is no clear sense of priorities that pose a common challenge to the whole team. This is even more common on virtual teams that include many different perspectives.

Example

IBToys listed these five issues as their make-or-break priorities:

- Meshing the two employee cultures between toy company and computer company so that the team works together
- Creating a product different from the competition
- Reducing the development costs for the project
- Utilizing existing resources of the companies
- Establishing identity in the marketplace

*V*The irtual Challenge

There will be two sets of issues to be defined. The first make-or-break issues are related to the project itself. But secondly, there will be make-or-break issues related to the team process as a whole and how it works together in a virtual environment.

YOUR TURN

From the ideas and challenges you generated in Step A, pick what you believe are the top five issues. Be sure to include any concerns you may have about how your team is currently functioning if you believe those concerns are of a "make-or-break" severity.

List your top five issues in the space below.

1.   4.

2.   5.

3.

Step C.
Problem solve top priorities

• **What it means:**
— A systematic process to generate creative solutions

• **How it works:**
— Frame the problem
— Define the root causes
— Expand options
— Narrow alternatives
— Choose a direction
— Analyze the pros and cons

The Idea

Once there is consensus on the top five issues, it is essential that the team designates time to address those issues. Depending upon the nature of the issues and the degree of urgency, it is usually best to schedule 2 to 4 hours on five different days to address each issue individually. Use electronic decision-making tools to support this process.

Problem Solving

Problem solving is a set of steps designed to generate creative solutions to issues confronting the team.

The process involves defining the problem, expanding options, narrowing alternatives and choosing direction.

While it is not necessary to adhere rigidly to every step in the process, following the steps ensures that the team will generate innovative ideas as well as reach agreement on where to focus its energies.

Most importantly, the process increases the likelihood that the team will invest its limited resources on the right problems.

Example
The IBToys team scheduled a creative problem-solving session to work on their first priority. They framed the problem as: our corporate culture clash precludes us from working together.

They defined the root causes as:

• We have a competitive view rather than a cooperative view.

• Distance and diversity have made it difficult to understand each other.

• We are more aware of our differences than our similarities.

They used brainstorming techniques to expand their options:

1. What if we all shared the same vision?

2. What if we meet together as a group in person occasionally?

3. What if we knew more about each other as whole persons by sharing our life stories?

4. How to find a way to work together that is less rigid than A Co. and more structured than B Co.

5. I like the idea of establishing a set of norms and structure that we all can agree to.

The *V*irtual Challenge

Solving problems in a virtual environment is more difficult because people are coming together from multiple functions and, possibly, multiple enterprises. When that happens, people tend to see what won't work, because the negatives will be glaring. For example, historical competition, compensation and cultural differences can at first appear to be impossible hurdles to overcome. It is critical to get people started on the right path by looking at what's possible rather than what's impossible.

This is a risky stage of the process. Members may feel afraid of getting their ideas shot down if trust has not been well established. Identifying challenges that may go against the group consensus requires taking a personal risk. It's often not a popular position to point out limitations. Trust and a positive environment are crucial.

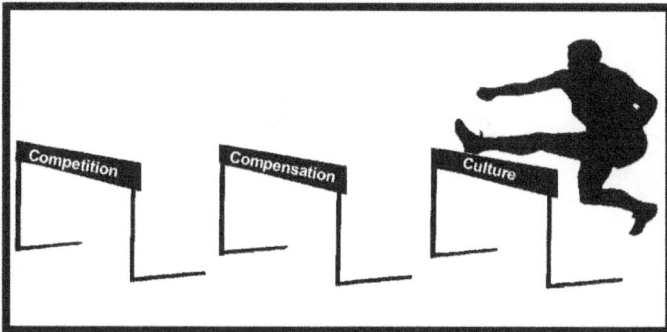

YOUR TURN

Break into groups of five. Pick one issue for each group to address. At a minimum, use the steps on the overhead to come up with a possible direction.

SKILL 2:
DEVELOP A COMMON PURPOSE AND PRINCIPLES

- **Definition:** Tapping into the deep aspiration of the team to make a difference
- **Benefits:**
  - — Lifts team members
  - — Grounds team members
- **Steps:**
  - A. Articulate the vision
  - B. Define the values
  - C. Agree on operating principles

Introduction

Developing a common purpose and set of common principles means tapping into the deep aspirations of the team to make a difference. Having a sense of purpose and a clear set of principles both elevates and anchors the team at the same time.

The purpose lifts the team sights to a higher aim while the principles ensure that the team stays grounded in a set of well-defined values. When a team has a common purpose, members articulate it enthusiastically and refer to it frequently.

People also understand the implications of the purpose and principles on their individual behavior and how the team functions. When teams have a common purpose and a set of operating principles, there are clear themes in their work and a sense of importance and excitement related to the work of the group.

During this process, it is best for the team to work at the same time so that all members feel part of the solutions and jointly agree. The synergy of the group working together on this important foundation stage will have better results than individuals working alone.

There are three steps involved with developing a common purpose and principles for the team:

Step A. Articulate the vision.
Step B. Define the values.
Step C. Agree on operating principles.

The *V*irtual Challenge

When we are working in a virtual environment, a clear purpose is an essential part of keeping people aligned. Additionally, operating principles must address how virtual teams can collaborate and communicate most effectively.

Adhering to these communication principles is especially important because in a virtual environment, it's more difficult to know if someone wasn't in the loop and didn't get certain information. Each individual needs to be committed to the principles and understand that they personally benefit when all members operate within the established operating norms.

Step A.
Articulate the vision

- **What it means:**
  - Creating a short, powerful statement describing the ideal end-state for your team
- **What it does:**
  - Reflects the furthest implications of the team
  - Mobilizes the team
  - Generates passion
- **How it works:**
  - Write a ten-word statement

The Idea

A vision reflects the future hopes and dreams of a team. It should describe the ideal end-state for your team and mobilize the team behind an exciting purpose.

An effective vision statement should:

- Be short and powerful.
- Communicate the ideal image of the future.
- Provide a primary focus.
- Generate passion in the group.
- Motivate team members to work consciously and unconsciously toward the vision.

A good test of a vision statement is whether or not you would like to have your picture taken next to it so that you could give it to your grandchildren to reflect how you invested your limited time on earth.

Without a strong vision statement, team members may be more focused on day-to-day tasks without a clear sense of the overall context and purpose.

A vision statement also becomes a benchmark for evaluating the actions of the group.

Example

An inspiring vision statement should provide optimism, clarify the future, reduce uncertainty and focus attention. It should be both strategic and emotional including ideas about change, goals and people. Use emotional words, metaphors and visual images to create the most powerful vision statement. Be as specific as possible.

The IBToys Company team created the following vision statement:

Creating a brighter future by inspiring, entertaining and educating children.

The *V*irtual Challenge

Creating a vision statement is a high-energy, interactive, spontaneous process. Whenever possible, use the technology that is the most transparent. Same time/ same place or same time/different place modules should be used for this step, because you need the synergy of active participation and the spontaneity that comes from real-time discussions. The more demand for spontaneity and interaction, the more demand there is for a rich communication experience. That is, the more levels of information we gain from our senses, the richer the communication experience.

YOUR TURN

In the space below, write an inspiring vision statement for your team. Try to keep the statement to less than 10 words.

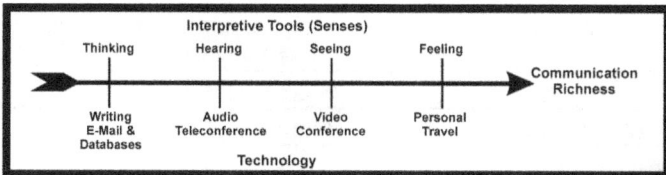

Interpretive Tools (Senses)			
Thinking	Hearing	Seeing	Feeling
Writing E-Mail & Databases	Audio Teleconference	Video Conference	Personal Travel

Communication Richness

Technology

Step B.
Define the values

- **What it means:**
  - — Agreeing on what is most important to the team
- **How it works:**
  - — Reach agreement on core values of the team
  - — Identify individual values
  - — Determine the match between individual and team values

The Idea

Values simply define what is important to the team and how it works together. Too often business has focused only on the end result, rather than the path taken to reach the end.

If the vision statement says where your team is going, values say you how you plan to get there. Values facilitate decision making by providing a foundation for sound judgment.

In the past 20 years, we have experienced dramatic shifts in the values driving organizations (Lippett):

From	To
• company growth	• customer growth
• competition	• teamwork
• closely held information	• openness
• exclusivity	• respect for differences
• internal focus	• social and environmental responsibility
• accumulation	• actualization
• quantity of work	• quality of life/balance

Example

Our team at IBToys was asked what was important to them in working together. Several common values emerged:

- Quality
- Support
- Communications
- Respect
- Interdependence
- Trust
- Success Oriented

The *V*irtual Challenge

Value shifts are taking place at different rates in different cultures. It is important not to impose the rate of change across different cultures. In the old model, we tried to impose our values and products on our customers. In the new model we act in concert with our "partner-customers" to develop the products and instill the values that make sense for both.

1950

Independence
Competitive
Secretive
Working Harder

2000

Interdependence
Collaborative
Open
Thinking Better

YOUR TURN

What is your perception of the most important values for your team?

Which values represent major changes for your organization over time?

Step C.
Agree on operating principles and norms

- **What it means:**
  - — Defining the illustrative norms and behaviors that put the values into action
- **How it works:**
  - — Translate each value into illustrative behaviors
  - — Select three to five behaviors that best describe the ideal environment for your team

The Idea
Defining the values is a good first step, but it is also necessary to agree on a set of operating principles that enable the team to measure whether or not behaviors are consistent with the values.

Each value should have a list of approximately five "norms" that put the values into action. Norms are the accepted and rewarded behaviors of the team. Stated simply, norms are the "way we do things around here."

These norms often become the oil that keeps the group functioning smoothly.

Example
The IBToys Team created a set of norms around the value of communications, as it related to working on workgroup technology.

- Team members are kept informed of important issues through database postings.
- We communicate openly, honestly, and directly.
- We receive and give on-going feedback that helps to improve performance.

- We communicate on-line with as much courtesy and respect as we would if talking face-to-face.
- We reply to E-Mail messages within 24 hours and check team databases at least once a day.

The *V*irtual Challenge

It is important to think about these norms as they relate to your context. In today's world "around here" can mean anywhere around the world. Yet our tendency is to define "here" as our immediate physical space.

For virtual teams, norms around communication, collaboration and involvement are especially important. Even when people have the technology to communicate on virtual teams, they often feel left out of the process. We will explore virtual communications more fully in Task III.

Creating norms for managing the inevitable fragments of communications, some that may happen off-line or informally, is a critical part of communicating success-fully in the virtual environment.

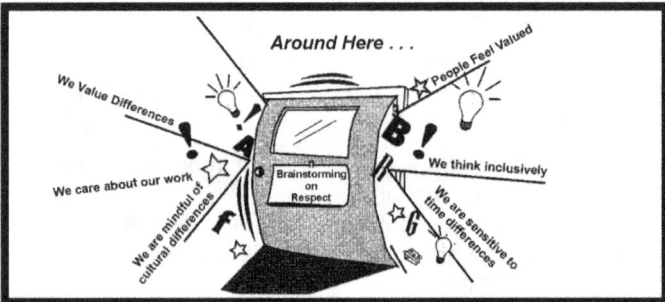

Around Here . . .

We Value Differences
People Feel Valued
We care about our work
We are mindful of cultural differences
Brainstorming on Respect
We think inclusively
We are sensitive to time differences

YOUR TURN

In the space below, write five norms for one of the values you chose for your team. Please include norms that relate to operating in a virtual world.

Value:

Norms:

1.

2.

3.

4.

5.

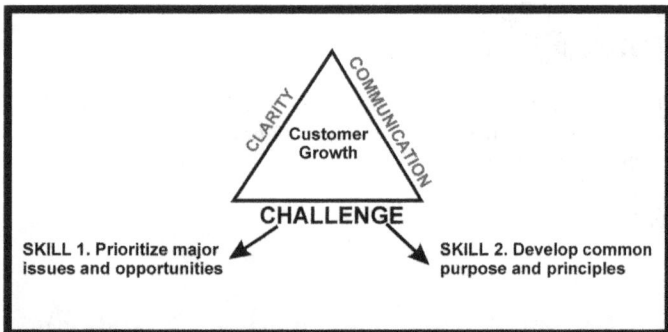

SKILL 1. Prioritize major issues and opportunities

SKILL 2. Develop common purpose and principles

Task I. Challenge Exercise

In this task, you learned two skills to challenge the performance of your team:

- Prioritize major issues and opportunities
- Develop common purpose and principles

Please review these two skills and decide what actions you can take in your team to challenge performance.

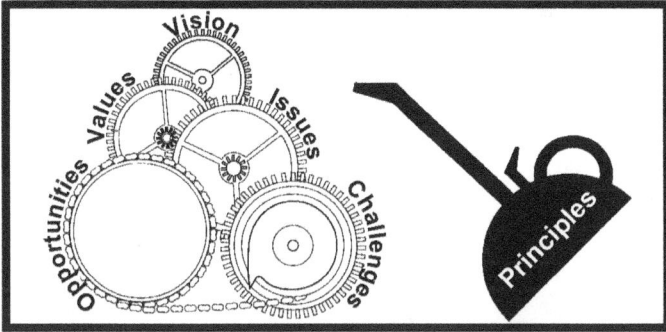

Task I. Summary

In this task you learned to create the foundation for challenging the performance of your team. You first conducted an internal and external scan of the environment to identify the key factors of change, creating challenges and opportunities for your team.

Within these major factors, you then identified the five make-or-break issues to help your team focus their efforts. You used problem-solving techniques to develop creative solutions to your top five key issues.

To establish a common framework for your team, it is important to establish a common purpose and set of principles. To align the team members to a common purpose you developed a vision statement that ignites team members' imagination for what might be. People can use this vision statement as a touchstone throughout the project.

Along with the vision you defined the team's values, keeping in mind the cultural and organizational differences among members. To ensure that the team is a well-oiled machine with all parts moving in the same direction, you agreed to a set of operating principles that define how you plan to work together. These principles are connected and supportive of the values and vision of the team.

Task II.
Clarify Direction

Key Ingredients:
- Alignment
- Integration
- Orchestration

Critical Skills:
3. Establish a plan
4. Define roles and responsibilities

Introduction

Clarifying direction means determining where the team is heading and how it is going to get there. By making the direction explicit, the whole team understands how their roles and responsibilities fit within the mission, goals and objectives of the team. Just as metal filings align in the direction of a strong magnet, so do all levels of an organization align when the direction is clearly understood. Clarifying direction makes it possible to integrate all functions in the organization and to orchestrate all the processes in the organization in order to achieve customer growth.

To Clarify Direction for your team you will learn two new skills:

Skill 3. Establish a plan

Skill 4. Define roles and responsibilities

Direction has to be crystal-clear at all levels of the organization for people to feel they are aligned with a single purpose. Ultimately, you would know that direction was clear if:

- everyone understood the vision, mission, goals, objectives, strategies and initiatives of the organization;
- everyone knew how their tasks, steps and responsibilities supported the vision, mission, goals, etc;
- all departments were working cross-functionally to achieve the business objectives;
- all processes led to customer growth.

In the previous section you defined the vision, values and norms that would guide how work would be done in your team. In this section, you will define the mission, goals, objectives, and roles that will clarify what needs to be done in order for your team to declare itself a high performing unit.

SKILL 3:
ESTABLISH A PLAN

- **Definition:** Setting reach objectives that the team can achieve if they work together
- **Benefits:**
  - — Provides a focal point
  - — Leverages collective competence
- **Steps:**
  - A. Define the mission
  - B. Develop the goals and objectives

Introduction

A poet once said, "A person's reach must exceed their grasp or what's a heaven for." Establishing a plan means setting "reach" objectives that the team can "grasp" only if they work together as a team. Effective leaders realize that the real goal is team performance rather than individual achievement. "Reach" objectives cannot be achieved by summing up the individual contributions of the team. "Reach" objectives require:

- Complementary skills,
- A larger purpose,
- Joint responsibility,
- Collective competence, and
- Mutual accountability.

Establishing a plan begins with defining the mission, because the mission is the focal point for all work. If the mission is off center or not compelling, then work will likely go astray.

The mission should provide a positive outlook for the future and a compelling rally point for the whole organization. It becomes a touchstone for each team member to refocus on the larger purpose when times get tough.

Establishing a plan involves two steps:

Step A. Define the mission.
Step B. Develop the goals and objectives.

The *V*irtual Challenge

While establishing a plan is a fairly routine procedure for same place/same time groups, it is less common in virtual teams. It seems that when we are geographically or organizationally dispersed, we are less likely to get common agreement on missions, goals and objectives.

Gaining agreement on missions, goals and objectives requires a rich communication experience. Team technology enables communication in a virtual environment, yet there is still a need to balance the use of the technology with face-to-face communication. Managing the communication continuum is a very important aspect of managing the virtual team process. Knowing when the team needs to meet in person versus when the technology can be used to greatest advantage is the challenge for the team leaders.

Step A.
Define the mission

- **What it means:**
  - Describing the products and/or services that define a team's reason for being
- **How it works:**
  - Understand your customer's productivity and profitability goals
  - Define your team's productivity and profitability goals
  - Write a statement that clearly and briefly captures both
  - Add statement to workgroup technology mission page

The Idea

A mission statement briefly describes the products and/ or services that constitute a team's reason for existence. The organizational or team mission statement in the ideal state is a collection of personal mission statements. It communicates what the team is expected to accomplish and establishes the focal point for all goals, objectives and strategies.

In the process of developing a mission statement, it can be helpful to collect customer and community perceptions of your mission. Like a vision statement, a mission statement should evoke feeling and passion. But a mission statement speaks in more detail about how the vision is accomplished.

A mission statement clarifies the:

- Team's purpose,
- Customer's needs,
- Team's uniqueness.

A comprehensive mission statement should incorporate productivity and profitability goals for the team and the customer. It should mobilize the whole team behind a clear focus.

Example
The IBToys mission statement:

To build on the individual success of our two companies in providing leading edge computer products to individuals and businesses and quality toys to our children.

- *The IBToys Co. is created as a joint profitable venture to develop a technologically advanced computer specifically created for children.*
- *The computer will be designed to facilitate learning, inspire creativity, and increase computer literacy among our youngest generation.*

The *V*irtual Challenge

In a virtual team, the mission statement should establish joint direction. Typically, organizational departments make sure they have a mission—temporary teams rarely do. But a shared mission is one element that allows a team to reach high performance early, particularly when teams form and disband quickly.

YOUR TURN

In the space below, answer the following questions.

What is the nature of your business?

How do you help your customers achieve their growth goals?

What are your strengths?

How are you unique?

Now synthesizing the answers to the questions above, formulate your view of your team or organization's mission:

Step B.
Develop the goals and objectives

- **What it means:**
    - Establishing direction, quantifiable milestones, and interdependencies
- **How it works:**
    - Write 5–7 goals that support your mission
    - Develop 3–5 measurable objectives that support each goal
    - Identify interdependencies and potential conflicts
    - Estimate resource requirements
    - Establish rewards for accomplishments

The Idea

Goals and objectives further solidify the direction of the team. An effective team normally has five to seven goals that support the mission. Goals are generally directional statements that define a particular set of tasks required to achieve the mission. As we think about setting goals we can remember the acronym SMART.

Goals are:

S	**S**pecific
M	**M**easurable
A	**A**chievable
R	**R**ealistic
T	**T**imed

Goals. Goals need to be specific action statements, providing clear direction of the task at hand. Goals should be measurable so that the team can assess and evaluate whether the goal has been achieved. Goals need to be challenging, but achievable. If a goal is too easy, it won't motivate. But a goal must be realistic or it will discourage.

Goals have a finite time frame with a beginning and an end. Some goals may take from six months to three years to accomplish. For teams that form for only three months, however, goals may take on a different time dimension. The time frame of goals should not be so long that team members become discouraged, yet long enough for significant strides to be made.

Objectives. Each objective should be related to accomplishing a particular goal. An objective is typically defined by time and amount and requires a shorter period of time than a goal.

Effective goals and objectives should identify where interdependencies are required between two or more team members or with other teams. They should clarify what each member is trying to accomplish and identify potential points of conflict.

All team members should be involved not only in setting goals and objectives but also in determining the measures for success and rewards for accomplishment.

Use the categories of product, process, people, workgroup technology and culture to check the completeness of your goals and to expand your objectives. You can use the chart on the next page to help you.

Example
Using the categories of process, people and technology the IB Toys team analyzed their project.

Process: They recognized a lack of processes designed to work cross-functionally. The team would have to build in processes to function both cross-functionally and cross-organizationally.

People: Team members from Company A were now reporting to leaders from Company B. The team needed to address these new relationships, and how to continue employee development in this context.

Technology: The team addresses the technology needed to work virtually.

The Virtual Challenge

Workflow management and scheduling software lend themselves to creating and tracking team goals and objectives. This technology supports the specificity, measurement and timed aspects of goals.

Team technology should be used to communicate the achievements, milestones, progress and results of each task to all members of the team. Each member should not only have access to the information, but should be encouraged to actively share task results. In other words, make the sharing of task results an active rather than a passive process.

Market Demands

People | Products | Processes | Technology | Culture

Customer Growth

YOUR TURN

In the space below, write down your view of your team goals.

Which goals will require coordination among team members and/or additional resources?

Write objectives for each goal.

SKILL 4:
DEFINE ROLES AND RESPONSIBILITIES

- **Definition:** Focusing on key results and clarifying division of responsibility and authority
- **Benefits:**
  — Defines expectations, reduces conflict, increases support
  — Increases accuracy and fairness of performance management
- **Steps:**
  A. Distribute tasks and accountabilities
  B. Define categories of information
  C. Describe the key events facing the team

Introduction

Roles and responsibilities focus on the key results to be achieved by each team member and make clear the division of responsibility and authority of each member. Some of the key roles in the team process might include:

- **Team Leader**—transmits information; interprets policies; communicates work details and management directives to the team; builds communication among team members; monitors and rewards team behavior; encourages risk taking; guides and shapes direction; resolves conflicts.

- **Team Facilitator**—schedules work and meetings; clarifies and restates goals and objectives; tests for consensus; keeps the team on track; organizes ideas; keeps the team on task during meetings; protects the supportive environment for ideas; doesn't take sides.

- **Team Process Observers**—have their fingers on the emotional pulse of the team. They are the "vibes coordinators." Process observers encourage participation; detect and confront any hidden agendas; assist in resolving conflict; encourage active listening; evaluate team processes.

- **Team Recorder**—takes the minutes of meetings and distributes a copy of them to each team member. On a virtual team, this role is handled electronically as part of the process.

- **Timekeeper**—sets time limits for meeting topics and monitors to keep the group on time.

- **Team members**—are prepared; participate; meet commitments; help resolve team conflicts when appropriate; accept and support consensus decisions of the team; get outside resources when needed; strive for quality work in self and others.

People who work interdependently need to share information and expectations in order to be committed to the team and its objectives.

Defining roles and responsibilities enables each team member to know what others are expected to do to meet team goals. By sharing information and negotiating expectations, conflicts are reduced and more easily resolved whenever there are differences in perception.

Clear roles and responsibilities also make it possible for team members to support each other more effectively. Finally, defining roles and responsibilities makes performance management more accurate and fair.

Defining roles and responsibilities includes three steps:

Step A. Distribute tasks and accountabilities.
Step B. Define categories of information.
Step C. Describe the key events facing the team.

The standard roles within a team operate differently when in a virtual environment. People who have functioned in a specific role for face-to-face teams often find themselves needing to learn a different set of skills when working on a virtual team. Each role will take on a slightly different spin. For example, the team facilitator ensures that team members are communicating and checks the virtual environment for issues requiring resolution. Communication is so critical in a virtual team that the importance of this team role is elevated to a higher level, and the team facilitator's role may overlap with the process observers.

On a virtual team, defining roles and responsibilities may present these special challenges:

- Evaluation is difficult because day-to-day performance is not observed.
- The person who leads the team may not be the boss.
- A person's role in a cross-functional team may not be the same as their job description.
- One person may be on five different teams at the same time.
- When a person has multiple bosses, all bosses tend to assume they have the person 100 percent.

When assigning roles on a virtual team, the tendency may be to take the easy route, such as letting all roles be handled at corporate or centrally. There is evidence to suggest, however, that assigning key roles to remote personnel has advantages.

When distributing accountability in virtual teams, interdependencies can be matrixed. This task requires thorough planning. There is more risk in this environment because it is more difficult to monitor progress. While virtual work does present considerable challenges, some technologies are available that make it possible to perform effectively. For example, effectively used databases capture work as it proceeds, allowing progress to be tracked.

Step A.
Distribute tasks and accountabilities

- **What it means:**
    - Creating logical groupings of tasks to be completed
- **How it works:**
    - Segment work categories based on roles and responsibilities
    - Assign all tasks fairly and equitably
    - Share leadership as well as mundane tasks

The Idea

All tasks within the team must be assigned. In a virtual team each member is dependent on the other members to hold up their end of the deal. For example, if one team member failed to post their progress into the database, other team members would have false information about interdependent tasks.

It is also important that tasks and types of work be assigned fairly and equitably. In any project there are always tasks that nobody enjoys doing but that have to be done—the "somebody's got to do it" task. It is critical that these be assigned fairly to prevent resentment. It may even be helpful to rotate those responsibilities so that the distasteful tasks are evenly distributed.

By the same token, resentment will be avoided if the favored tasks are also spread around. By assigning tasks equitably, all team members stay motivated and feel they have an important contribution to make.

Every objective may have several tasks. Each task should include:

- an estimate of person days required for completion,
- who is responsible for completion,
- the start and end dates for completion.

By estimating person days per task, it is possible to distribute work fairly and to decide what can and can't be done.

Example
Our team from IBToys worked by consensus to determine who in the team would be the leader, facilitator, observer, recorder and timekeeper. Once those responsibilities were determined, the marketing team went about developing a detailed description of every task and responsibility required to meet their goals and objectives.

The group decided to rotate the leadership within the marketing team so that both organizations would have representative leadership responsibilities.

Even though some of their team members lived and worked in Japan, all tasks were assigned equitably. They made sure not to assume that even though someone seemed far away, they wouldn't want to be deeply involved.

The team incorporated each member's roles and responsibilities into their biosketch included in the Team Room participant profile.

The Virtual Challenge

In a virtual environment it is very easy for things to slip through the cracks. Often these missing pieces may not be noticed until the very end of the project, creating delays at a critical point. The chart of activities, schedules and workflow management may require a higher degree of detail than in a single office environment to ensure that all tasks are anticipated and included. Individuals need to maintain awareness of interdependencies with remote team members. When working on multiple teams, it becomes the individual's responsibility to balance the workload.

Task Cards

YOUR TURN

In the space below, take one objective and list the tasks required to achieve it. Then assign the tasks to the appropriate person. Estimate the number of person days needed to accomplish the task. Assign a timeline for each task. The following chart may be useful.

Objective _____

_____

_____

Tasks   Who Is Responsible   Person Days   Due Date

_____

_____

_____

_____

_____

_____

_____

_____

_____

_____

_____

_____

_____

_____

Step B.
Define categories of information

- **What it means:**
  - — Verifying that all tasks relate to stated goals
- **How it works:**
  - — Evaluate the kinds of information shared in the team
  - — Compare information and activity with goals, tasks and objectives
  - — Add new goals, tasks or objectives if necessary

The Idea

Defining categories of information is a check step to verify that all of the team's activities relate to the stated goals, objectives and tasks. This step enables the team to determine how much of its work is deductive and how much is inductive.

If most of the issues you talk about as a team are not related to the mission, goals and objectives, that indicates that either the planning process is incomplete or there is a lot of wasted effort or reactionary activity.

When teams categorize the information they share as a group, it enables them to learn about what's important and, if necessary, to add additional goals. Ideally, defining the categories of work also improves the ways in which teams share information.

Example

A few weeks into the working phase of their project, the IB Toys leaders took the time to evaluate the work done to date by reviewing the communications from the subteams. They looked to see that the discussion, activity and information entered into the database was aligned with the goals, objectives and mission of the team.

Through this review process, the leaders realized that one group had gotten side-tracked from an event that had happened.

A group from the U.S. engineering team was assigned to work together with engineers in Japan to establish relations with a new manufacturer to supply micro-chips for the new computer. Reviewing the communications among the team members showed that most of the discussion and research to date had been focused on a fire that occurred at a competitor's chip manufacturer and how that might affect the market. Although this information was of relevance, the amount of time being spent on this issue was disproportional, indicating that this subteam had drifted away from their primary task.

The Virtual Challenge

In a virtual environment the challenge is to keep everyone on the team up-to-date on decisions being made and changes happening in the project. If remote members of the team do not check in frequently, decisions made by other group members could affect the remote person's task. Once a team defines its tasks, they need a structured way to continuously reaffirm these tasks, goals and objectives. Posting minutes from all meetings and keeping work products on shared databases are two ways of sharing information.

YOUR
TURN

Reflect upon the issues you discuss as a team. Do they all relate to your goals and objectives? If not, do you need to add goals or do you need to reduce the amount of time spent on non-goal-related activity?

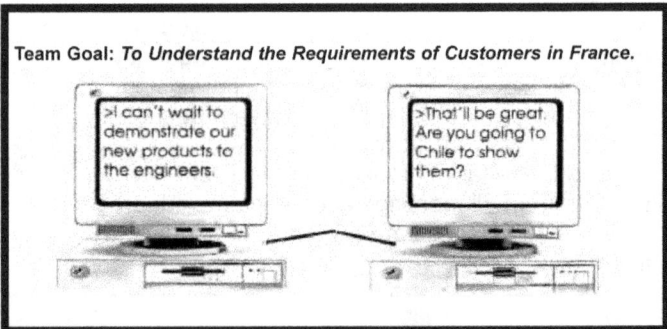

Team Goal: *To Understand the Requirements of Customers in France.*

>I can't wait to demonstrate our new products to the engineers.

>That'll be great. Are you going to Chile to show them?

Step C.
Describe the key events facing the team

- **What it means:**
  - — Highlighting critical events that will determine success or failure for the team
- **How it works:**
  - — Identify two to three major events
  - — Agree on deadlines
  - — Establish milestones

The Idea

In achieving your objectives there are normally events or milestones that help team members focus on their work. These milestones usually revolve around review or delivery of certain work. This step serves as a reality check on interdependencies. Key questions usually arise regarding the necessary deadlines for the team. This includes deadlines for objectives, goals and the overall mission.

Example

The marketing team of IBToys had their six-month deadline for developing a marketing plan. However, each task was assigned a benchmark deadline to help them stay on track to meet the six-month goal. They also established that certain tasks had to be completed before they could move on. For example, before they could knowledgeably create focus group questions, they needed to familiarize themselves with current trends in computer technology regarding voice-activated software and multi-media learning models. The group also got feedback from engineering and design teams about their needs for the market research data. All of the deadlines and event milestones were entered into the central electronic project management calendar. Then, team members could see the gaps and conflicts. After adjusting the schedules to all members' satisfaction, they set about their individual tasks.

The Virtual Challenge

Tracking and scheduling software can facilitate the process of setting team milestones, but it is only as successful as the people who use it. In a virtual environment team leaders must find a way to enforce discipline among members to update the team schedule. This can be a real challenge. People tend to be gung-ho in the beginning when performing work on a new tool, but over time they may get distracted by other tasks and fail to keep the information updated. Incentives, flags, periodic checks and good role modeling are a few ways leaders can help facilitate this discipline.

**YOUR
TURN**

*What are the events or milestones on which your team
must focus? What are the deadlines?*

Trip across the
country milestones:
California
Colorado
Ohio
Pennsylvania
New York

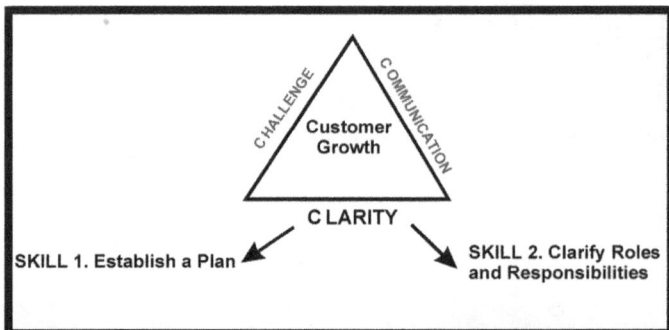

CHALLENGE · COMMUNICATION

Customer Growth

C LARITY

SKILL 1. Establish a Plan ← → SKILL 2. Clarify Roles and Responsibilities

Task II. Clarity Exercise

In this task you learned two skills to help your team clarify its direction:

• Establish a plan
• Clarify roles and responsibilities

Please review these two skills and decide what actions you can take in your team to clarify direction.

Task II. Summary

In this task you learned to clarify the direction for your team. This involved creating a plan, assigning responsibilities and learning how workgroup technologies could move your team through the stages of development.

To establish a plan you first defined a mission. The mission for a team is more concrete than the vision statement you articulated in Task I. Nonetheless, the mission is aligned and in agreement with the vision.

In addition to the mission, you developed a set of goals and objectives for your team. This gave you a road map to get from A to B by breaking down the project into smaller portions.

Once it was clear what had to be done, then it was time to define who was to do the work. First you distributed tasks and assigned accountability—making sure that each function and task was assigned fairly and equitably.

By defining categories of information, you established a check to make sure that all the work is related to the goals, objectives and tasks.

Finally, you described the key events facing the team, setting the milestones of what had to be done and when. This step made interdependencies and scheduling conflicts more apparent, allowing diverse team members to work together effectively.

Task III.
Communicate, Communicate, Communicate

Key Ingredients:
- Attitudes
- Behaviors
- Skills

Critical Skills:
5. Value differences
6. Use interpersonal skills
7. Demonstrate leadership

Introduction

If there is one critical ingredient for team success it is the ability to communicate. Effective communication is a combination of attitudes, behaviors and skills. Our attitudes toward other members of the team play a major role in how the team performs.

If team members are genuine, respectful and positive toward other members, a climate is created in which open, honest and direct communications can take place. When there is open communication, trust levels go up in the group. People begin to think interdependently, involve others in decisions that affect them and look for ways to support each other. When there is open communications, people seek out multiple perspectives and give constructive feedback. Open communications, however, require positive attitudes from team members. Attitudes communicate a great deal in a team setting.

Our behaviors toward other team members also play a major role in how the team performs. For example:

- Do we act in ways that are consistent with what we say is important?
- Do we fulfill the commitments and promises we make to each other?
- Are new team members selected for their skill vs. their political aptitude?
- Do team members protect confidentiality agreements?
- Do we engage in constructive confrontation?
- Does every team member do real work?
- Do we spend time together?
- Does the team recognize exceptional contributions by other team members?
- Do we engage the appropriate team members in work activities, wherever they may be located?
- Do we maintain an active presence for each other in our shared virtual workspace?

The answers to these questions send powerful messages to the team. It's an old cliché, but it's true—actions speak louder than words. When we think about communications in teams, therefore, we need to pay as much attention to our behaviors as we do to our words.

Leadership
Leadership skills also play a major role in how the team performs. Successful leaders need to lead, facilitate teamwork and manage team communications. But today, they have to also be able to do it in a virtual world. This requires a new set of skills.

Trust, an Essential Element of Team Development
When a team performs well, its members have a strong level of trust in each other. Openness, acceptance and security create trust. Each member of a team can enhance trust within the group or create barriers to trust. When working in a team, build trust by fostering the following characteristics in yourself and others:

T	**Tolerance**—Accept the ideas of others with minimal criticism. If you disagree, keep your critique focused on the idea, not the person.
R	**Responsibility**—Keep commitments and don't make promises you can't keep.
U	**Understanding**—Allow for differences in others. Communicate clearly to ensure that others can understand your ideas. Be open to feedback and give support when needed.
S	**Share ideas**—Be honest in your communication and include others.
T	**Togetherness**—Don't create hidden agendas or cliques within the group. Spend time with team members outside the work environment, when possible. Have fun.

Developing good communications for team success involves three skills:

Skill 5. Value Differences

Skill 6. Use Interpersonal Skills

Skill 7. Demonstrate Leadership

$\mathcal{V}$ The irtual Challenge

While attitudes, behaviors, and skills all send messages in traditional teams, they take on even greater importance in virtual teams where people are unable to see each other face-to-face or spend time together. The virtual team environment adds new communication and leadership demands on each team member.

Formally through education and informally through social interactions we have learned a set of skills to communicate with others. But although we can use these skills as a foundation for communicating virtually, a new set of skills is also required, and many of our old skills will no longer apply.

Today, we take for granted the skills needed to talk on the phone to someone who we cannot see. Imagine the awkwardness and potential confusion of people learning these skills for the first time when the telephone was invented. Much like the telephone pioneers learning to speak to each other over a wire, today's virtual teams are learning new skills to communicate in a virtual world.

Sailing the Seven C's

Confidentiality
Commitment
Confrontation
Competitiveness
Consistency
Computers
Contribution

SKILL 5:
VALUE DIFFERENCES

- **Definition:** Thinking inclusively and respecting other points of view
- **Benefits:**
  - — Develops new insights
  - — Deepens understanding
  - — Overcomes lack of visual cues in Virtual Team environment
- **Steps:**
  - A. Understand personal profile
  - B. Understand team member profiles
  - C. Understand how differences contribute to team effectiveness

---

Introduction

Valuing differences means thinking inclusively and respecting other points of view. In this age of divisiveness, the ability to understand and value differences is a crucial challenge to all of us. When differences are valued, teams are more likely to hear multiple perspectives and to develop new insights on old problems. Also, different perspectives from different parts of the organization can be leveraged to achieve higher overall team vision and perspective.

In order to be effective, teams not only need to have complementary skills and styles, they also need to value the differences in what each team member brings to the team. People who know themselves and others well are better able to communicate than those who have big blind spots regarding their own behavior and a lack of insight into others.

Each personality has its own strengths. Persons with different personality styles may find some jobs more enjoyable and less stressful. In the same way, persons with different personality styles may interact and work with workgroup technology in different ways. Respecting the differences of other work styles builds trust and support among team members. Actual job performance, however, is based more on skills and abilities than on personality style.

For this skill, we will use the *Insight Inventory** as a tool for deepening your understanding of yourself and others. The Insight Inventory is a tool for measuring one dimension of individual uniqueness and personality. It will give you insight into your personality strengths and how you behave in two different worlds—your work environment and your home-personal life.

There are three steps to using the *Insight Inventory*:

Step A. Understand personal profile.
Step B. Understand team member profiles.
Step C. Understand how differences contribute to team effectiveness.

The Virtual Challenge

In a virtual team, you may encounter the added challenge of needing to value differences of different organizations and even different cultures. Not only will there be personality differences, but differences in organizational and cultural protocol. For example, the concept of "on time" means very different things in different cultures. In the United States, 5 to 10 minutes late is tolerated as being on time. In other cultures, the accepted tolerance for lateness may be as much as an hour. Understanding and respecting these types of differences can be a real challenge.

*Available through HRD Press, 800-822-2801, www.hrdpress.com

Step A.
Understand your personal profile

- **What it means:**
  — Defining style preferences
- **How it works:**
  — Complete the Insight Inventory
  — Record scores
  — Understand implications and possibilities in a virtual environment

The Idea

The *Insight Inventory* is designed to help you learn more about yourself and the unique personality you have. People who know themselves well are more able to work with others. The *Insight Inventory* measures four ways people use their personality. Each style has two opposite extremes, or ways of behaving. A score in either direction is okay. There is no right or wrong style. Your scores simply indicate the ways of behaving you prefer to use most of the time.

The *V*irtual Challenge

Our personal workstyle may be very different in a virtual environment than in a face-to-face environment. We may be indirect and shy verbally when face-to-face, yet in the safety of a remote location through the written word, we may become much more direct.

Understanding how our styles differ in a virtual environment is an important step to understanding ourselves.

YOUR TURN

After you have completed the Insight Inventory, *record your scores in the middle column. Remember the scale runs from 8 to 48.*

Your Score
8 to 48

Indirect		Direct
Reserved		Outgoing
Urgent		Steady
Unstructured		Precise

Sally in a Meeting — "Sally, please speak up. Nobody can hear you." — Sally on-line

Step B.
Understand team member profiles

- **What it means:**
  - — Figuring out the best way to relate to other team members
- **How it works:**
  - — Compare your results to other team member results
  - — Identify those with similar styles to you, and those with different styles from you
  - — Identify ways that you could flex your style to achieve better results

The Idea

Just as it is important to understand your own profile, it is also important to understand the respective profiles of your team members. Effective teams have a large range of style differences that serve as complementary strengths within the group. Other points of view, other business plans and other perspectives can also create hurdles for us to get over.

People who have similar styles initially get along great. It is as if they both found someone who thinks and acts much like themselves. Problems can arise, however, when they find they both want to "tell" the other what to do, or neither one wants to take charge, etc.

Opposite styles can work well together when they respect and value each other's differences because they bring different perspectives to creative problem solving and decision making.

Leadership studies indicate that successful leaders are people who have developed skills in flexing their personality styles to match the situation.

The Virtual Challenge

It is particularly important to understand other team member profiles when working in a virtual team. When we interact with people face-to-face, we receive many cues from the other person. Some of these signals we may notice consciously, many others we receive as input in an unconscious way. Facial expressions, body movements, tone of voice and vocal inflections all provide many cues to understanding how the other person is reacting, feeling and interpreting what we say during the course of a conversation.

In a virtual team environment where much of the communication may be only in written form, these cues are no longer available to us. In this environment it is more difficult to detect problems, and people are more likely to let things fester when at a distance.

Having a greater understanding of each team members' personality and style can bridge the gap by providing us with concrete information that we then use to anticipate how someone might react. If they do respond in a way that is unexpected, we also have a reference to understand why they may have reacted that way.

Trust comes into play when working with personal profiles. People need to trust each other before they feel willing to reveal personal information.

The *Insight Inventory** can be a helpful tool, but we don't generally think of people in terms of numbers. It is important to create an understanding of the context and relevance of the information gained from the profile.

These scores will become more relevant if included in a contextual understanding of who the person is. Perhaps allow team members to make a five-minute video or audio clip about themselves that can be accessed in the virtual environment. Or each person can share a personal story. In this way, the profiles will have an interpretive frame of reference.

Other activities that enrich our understanding of others include sharing business plans and group learning about cultural differences.

*available from HRD Press, 800-822-2801, www.hrdpress.com

**YOUR
TURN**

Pick someone on your team whom you know quite well.

Guess what their scores are on the four scales. Use the table below to record your estimates.

My Guess at a Team Member's Score
(8 to 48)

Indirect		Direct
Reserved		Outgoing
Urgent		Steady
Unstructured		Precise

Team Member's Actual Score
(8 to 48)

Indirect		Direct
Reserved		Outgoing
Urgent		Steady
Unstructured		Precise

Step C.
Understand how differences contribute to team effectiveness

- **What it means:**
  - — Seeing differences as strengths
- **How it works:**
  - — Develop a team chart
  - — Calculate the range within each category
  - — Look for ways to utilize differences to achieve higher performance

The Idea

Teams work best when they have a broad variety of styles and can build on those differences in a positive way.

- Teams need people who get their way indirectly through strategy and careful planning, and people who get their way directly by taking charge and pushing for action.
- Teams need diplomats, as well as drivers.
- Teams need people who direct their energies inward to the world of ideas and thought, and people who direct their energy outward toward people and activities.
- Teams need people who think their way through situations, as well as people who talk their way through situations.
- Teams need people who burn energy in a fast-paced and restless manner, and people who burn energy in an even-paced, consistent manner.
- Teams need a sense of urgency, as well as a steadying influence.

- Teams need people who prefer to act first and attend to detail later, and people who strive to have their world very planned and predictable.
- Teams need "big picture" players, and precise players.

High performing teams understand how each member's style preferences can contribute to team effectiveness. Leveraging differences means mapping the unique skills and abilities of each team member to the requirements of the job at hand.

We can also leverage multi-organizational or multi-cultural differences. Members of a different organization may be more suited to certain functions within the team. Leveraging cultural differences can provide teams with strength and diversity when competing in a global economy.

Example
The engineers on the IBToys team had very different styles of working, thinking and communicating than the marketing team members.

Engineers tended to be very detail-oriented and needed an even-paced, structured work environment.

The marketing people were big picture thinkers; they were a little short on the details but high on energy.

The marketing people were uncomfortable communicating in writing where they could not accent their communication with gestures and verbosity. Likewise, the engineers were uncomfortable having on-line discussions in real time, preferring to compose their responses thoughtfully.

The team leaders leveraged the differences between these two groups by allowing the marketing people to have real time meetings, enhanced with video and audio. The minutes were distributed to the engineering people so that they could digest the information at their own pace and respond.

The Virtual Challenge

Personal communication strengths and weaknesses will have different effects in a virtual environment. A shy person or a humorous person may not translate well in a virtual environment.

Certain communication styles may not lend themselves to a virtual environment while other styles may be enhanced.

There may be language differences within cross-cultural teams. Deciding on a primary language for communication and using graphics or icons can help overcome these communication hurdles.

Leaders need to be sensitive to these differences and leverage the strengths and weaknesses among team members by creating a mixture of communication opportunities. An equity of opportunity for different styles of communication can leverage these communication differences.

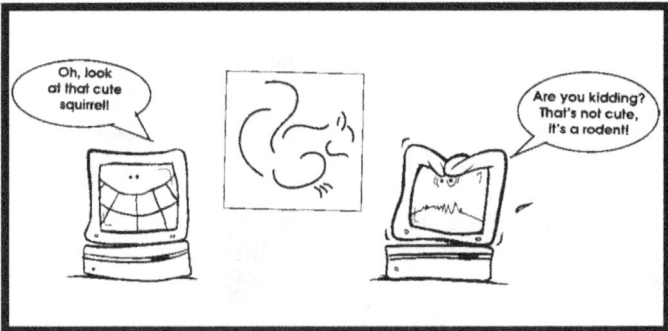

YOUR TURN

In the following chart, record the scores of all your team members so that you can understand how differences can contribute to team effectiveness.

Team Member Name	Indirect/ Direct	Reserved/ Outgoing	Urgent/ Steady	Unstructured/ Precise

What are some ways you can turn different business perspectives or cultural perspectives into opportunities for your team?

SKILL 6:
USE INTERPERSONAL SKILLS

- **Definition:** Developing and maintaining constructive relationships with other people
- **Benefits:**
  — Builds a base of understanding
  — Minimizes stresses
- **Steps:**
  A. Listen
  B. Question
  C. Demonstrate understanding
  D. Give your perspective/Disclose who you are
  E. Manage conflict

Introduction

Interpersonal communication is the ability to develop and maintain constructive relationships with other people. The way we deal with each other in relationships affects our health, our success, and many other dimensions of our lives. It certainly affects our relationships at work with associates, customers, and our ability to be a team player.

Skills in interpersonal communication can be used any time you are interacting with another person. Being able to communicate successfully requires knowing what both you and the other person are experiencing at any given moment and understanding how and when to provide a clear response or viewpoint.

Demonstrating understanding, also called empathy, is the single most important skill to use when you are trying to help another person, whether as a supervisor, co-worker, team member or friend.

Many of the interpersonal skills that have served us well in our lives need to be supplemented with new skills when we enter into a virtual work environment.

Mastering interpersonal skills for working on physical and virtual teams not only will enable you to develop positive relationships, but also will help you to minimize the stress of negative ones. Poor interpersonal communication can be one of the greatest sources of stress in our lives. Poor communications in a virtual team can create resentments, sabotage and failure of the team to reach its goal.

There are five steps to developing good interpersonal skills

Step A. Listen
Step B. Question
Step C. Demonstrate understanding
Step D. Give your perspective/Disclose who you are
Step E. Manage conflict

The *V*irtual Challenge

These skills are particularly critical on virtual teams where we are not able to pick up the cues of non-verbal communication and people may not interact with each other for extended periods of time.

How do you "listen" virtually? In a virtual environment, interpersonal communication often requires some new skills. It might be helpful to have activities in the beginning when the stakes are not so high. Social or fun activities that allow people to gain comfort and confidence with the technology can build a foundation for successful communication when the stakes get higher.

Step A.
Listen

- **What it means:**
  - — Hearing and interpreting verbal cues
- **How it works:**
  - — Resist distractions
  - — Suspend judgment
  - — Recall the content
  - — Reflect upon the meaning
  - — Reflect upon the volume, tone, pace, or writing style
  - — Paraphrase the content

The Idea

Listening means hearing and interpreting the written and verbal cues a person presents to you. Often someone will set the stage for you, present a topic, and then say what is most important to them. If you get caught up in the general topic, you may not receive the most significant message.

At a fundamental level, it is important for everyone to have a sense of how much time they spend listening and how much time they spend talking. Listening is particularly important in a group situation because our interactions are broadcast to all group members as well as the team leader.

Often we get so excited to communicate our ideas that we formulate our thought about what we're going to say next, instead of actively listening to the person speaking. Telltale signs of someone not listening are:

- Interrupting;
- Finishing or cutting off the end of someone's sentence;
- Jumping to another topic that has no connection to what's just been said.

In listening to the content of a message and how it is sent, and in trying to avoid some of the pitfalls of non listening, here's how you can gather more complete and accurate information through active listening:

- **Resist distractions**—Clear your mind so that you can focus on what the speaker is saying.

- **Be open**—Have a curiosity about what the other person's idea might be. It could be terrific!

- **Suspend judgment (at least temporarily)**—Hold your criticism at least until after the person has communicated their whole idea or thought.

- **Recall the content**—Review and summarize what is being communicated.

- **Reflect upon the meaning**—Make connections between what is being said with what you know. How does it relate to other ideas?

- **Reflect upon the volume, tone, pace and word choices**—These often provide additional meaning to the words.

- **Paraphrase the content**—Reflect back to the person your understanding of what they just said. This demonstrates that you were listening and shows respect for the speaker.

- **Take notes**—This will help you focus, take in what's being said, and have a reference to reflect back on. It also shows that you are listening.

Attending, observing and listening are a group of skills that really work best when used together. They provide a solid foundation for communication. These skills will keep you from straying from an accurate understanding of the other person's experience.

The Virtual Challenge

How do we listen virtually? In a virtual setting, written cues can come from the length of sentences, type style, type size, word choice and use of non letter forms or graphics.

Not only do we need to "listen" for these written cues, we need to be sensitive to how our communications are interpreted by others. For example, one manager in Japan was offended when a North American manager sent an E-Mail in bold, capitalized letters. The Japanese manager interpreted the selection of type face as shouting.

It takes a great deal of discipline in a virtual setting to "hear" all the cues. We need to take the time to read fully another's communication (not just skim it), and we also may need to read between the lines.

YOUR TURN

Ask team members to share their perspective about a problem the team is facing. Try to paraphrase what each person said. Ask the team member if your listening response was complete and accurate.

Step B.
Question

- **What it means:**
  - — Using thoughtful inquiry to obtain a clear understanding
- **How it works:**
  - — Ask direct questions if you want short answers
  - — Ask open-ended questions if you want to encourage others to respond
  - — Don't ask leading questions

The Idea

Asking questions is obtaining a clear understanding of key issues and concerns using thoughtful inquiry. By asking appropriate questions, you can uncover critical information and get people involved when ownership is important. Questions come in three basic varieties:

Open questions—encourage others to talk and share their understanding of a topic. These questions cannot be answered in a few words; they may often require lengthy replies. Example: "What do you think about John's work?"

Direct questions—can be answered in a word or a phrase. They help you focus the communication and obtain specific data, but also may result in limited information. Example: "Where do you work?"

Leading questions—obstruct communication by suggesting a desired response within the question. They do not contribute to effective information gathering. Example: "You do like working here, don't you?"

The Virtual Challenge

In a virtual setting, questions are generally posted to the world, allowing anyone to answer. You may not know who to ask a particular question, so you can ask anyone. This can be very helpful, but the challenge is making sure the person most likely to know the information sees the question and takes the time to answer it. And reconciling multiple answers to a single question can lead to further inquiry or negotiation.

**YOUR
TURN**

*Ask a team member an open, a direct, and a leading
question.*

Open:

Direct:

Leading:

What were the differences in responses?

Step C.
Demonstrate understanding

- **What it means:**
    - — Expressing your comprehension of the other person's point of view
- **How it works:**
    - — Think it out first
    - — Paraphrase, don't parrot
    - — Keep it short
    - — Use words the other person will understand

The Idea

Demonstrating understanding is the ability to express your comprehension of the other person's point of view. By demonstrating understanding, you show the other person that you received their message. At the same time, you build rapport, confidence and, ultimately, trust.

The skills used in demonstrating understanding can be applied when you want or need to:

- verify what you have heard,
- defuse negative feelings,
- be helpful,
- establish a cooperative relationship.

Demonstrating understanding involves formulating a response and responding—by stating the content, feeling, and/or message you have heard, read or observed. Here are a few points to remember about the process:

- Think it out first. Ask yourself, "Is this what the person is really saying?"
- Paraphrase, don't echo or parrot.
- Keep it short.
- Use words the other person will understand, particularly when dealing with someone with a different language.

Example

Here is a series of E-Mail messages between a disgruntled team member and the team leader. See if you can notice how the team leader demonstrates understanding that helps diffuse the anger.

Team Member: I always give my best, but Joe got the job that I wanted. How come!@!#!????

Team Leader: It's true that you are doing very well, but Joe is doing well, too. He also has experience that you don't have. I think you are qualified, but Joe is more qualified in this area.

Team Member: I'm just so discouraged. I really wanted that job.

Team Leader: I can understand how disappointed you are, but improving your attitude could help you in the long run.

Team Member: I know. I'd better get it together.

*V*irtual Challenge
The

Demonstrating understanding is particularly important in a virtual team environment. Because there are no visual cues to aid in communication, it is helpful to reflect back your understanding of what the other person said. In this way, you have a way to check that what you think the other person said is really what they meant. This is not an intuitive process for most of us. We have to artificially complete the understanding loop to make sure we are more specific and clear about our communication. If understanding is missing, the risk of problems escalating and festering increases dramatically.

YOUR TURN

*After a team meeting, one worker says to another,
"I just don't know what to do first. I have so many things to
do I'm not sure where to begin. Everyone is so impatient."
Answering as if you were the co-worker, write your
understanding response below.*

Step D.
Give your perspective/
Disclose who you are

- **What it means:**
    — Presenting your view in an honest, straightforward and clear manner
- **How it works:**
    — Organize your viewpoint
    — Present your viewpoint
    — Demonstrate understanding of the reaction to your viewpoint

The Idea

Giving your perspective is presenting your views in an honest, straightforward and clear manner. Some of the most common reasons for giving your viewpoint are to:

- Tell others what you think of their behavior or performance;
- Get feedback on your perspective;
- Show others you either agree or disagree with them;
- Communicate your expectations; and
- Persuade others that your idea, product or service is valid.

The goal is not just to state your opinion, but to have it understood. In order to accomplish that goal, you will need to:

- Organize your viewpoint—set your goals, formulate your statement and then evaluate it for clarity and roadblock-causing language.

- Present your viewpoint—orient the listener to what you are saying and speak clearly and at a comfortable pace.
- Demonstrate understanding of the reaction to your viewpoint—this will give you cues to what's been heard or not heard.

The Virtual Challenge

Giving feedback, perspectives and disclosing who you are in a virtual environment is a higher risk activity than in a normal office setting because the communication is primarily in writing and therefore permanent and public. This increases personal accountability because whatever is said is subject to great scrutiny.

In addition, the chances of having communication read out of context is increased in a virtual setting. The communication is interpreted by the person who reads it. One person may interpret a feedback statement with neutrality while another may interpret it with sarcasm. It is important to communicate with sensitivity to these issues.

Beware of communicating in a facetious manner in a virtual environment. Without the verbal cues that let others know we are being facetious, your communication will likely be interpreted literally. It's best to play it straight for the sake of clarity than to risk misinterpretation.

Disclosing who you are is particularly difficult when communicating in a second language. Be sensitive to team members' primary and secondary language.

YOUR TURN

Write down your viewpoint regarding a situation in your team. In your viewpoint, try to include how you feel and why you feel that way, an example that helps the other person know exactly what you mean, and a statement that communicates what actions you wish the person would take to change his or her behavior and/or how you wish the situation would improve.

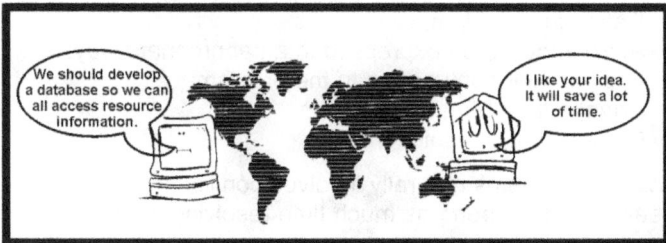

Step E.
Manage conflict

- **What it means:**
  - — Resolving differences in a way that results in a win-win outcome
- **How it works:**
  - — Identify values
  - — Expand alternatives
  - — Select the best alternative

The Idea

Managing conflict is a resolution of differences that provides for a win-win outcome by incorporating at least some values (needs and desires) of all parties to the conflict.

Conflict management should be used when you need another person's cooperation to carry out the solution to a problem. It's also useful when imposing your views would be counter-productive.

It will be difficult to manage conflicts if team members do not share a common set of agreements about working together and resolving conflicts. Team members need to be willing to:

- Listen openly;
- Focus on the problem, not the personalities;
- Define the problem;
- Allow anger to be expressed in an appropriate way;
- Look at their contribution to the problem;
- Change their behavior;
- Commit to the resolution.

Working in teams naturally involves conflict. In fact, young teams tend to spend as much time resolving conflict as they do actually working on the task. Just as the differing styles provide creative strength through diversity, so can they create conflict.

The Team Observer should be sensitive to the presence of underlying conflicts that may be brewing in both the physical and virtual environment. Addressing these conflicts early in the process prevents damage caused from undermining behavior and hidden agendas that damage team morale. The Team Observer can request a meeting/discussion among the parties in conflict and include the Team Leader and Facilitator.

A practical way to negotiate through a conflict involves three processes:

- **Identify values**—analyze your values and the values of others involved.
- **Expand alternatives**—brainstorm solutions that might satisfy each value.
- **Select the best alternative**—the solution that satisfies the most values.

There are two possible outcomes of conflict management:

- **Compromise**—some of the values of each party are satisfied in the solution.
- **Merging**—all of the values of each party are satisfied in the solution.

The best compromise satisfies, at a minimum, the values that are most critical to the parties involved. Any effective conflict negotiation considers and respects the values of all, and focuses on similarities in a viewpoint as well as on differences.

Sometimes conflict arises through basic behavior problems. The Team Leader and Team Facilitator can call a closed meeting to work together with the individual to change the problem behaviors. In this process, the leaders need to communicate, specifically and clearly, to the problem team member:

- Specific details about the problem behavior,
- Effects of the behavior on the team,
- The preferred action or behavior,
- Specific consequences if the behavior continues.

The irtual Challenge

In a virtual setting, conflict often goes underground. It is easier to share feelings within physical teams than when working virtually. You may not realize that a person is upset, but performance may drop without you knowing why. It requires the recognition of cues not previously aware of and to check with the other person regularly.

Team members need to be encouraged to let others know when they are upset. In a face-to-face setting, people have non-verbal ways of letting others know they are angry. In a virtual environment, these subtle cues are not as available. It may require learning new skills to be more aware of feelings and communicate openly and directly about dissatisfaction.

YOUR TURN

Select a situation in which effective conflict management skills would be beneficial. Briefly describe the situation, list the values of the parties involved, list some options that might be considered workable solutions, and evaluate the options by using the following chart:

Values	Option 1	Option 2	Option 3	Option 4
1				
2				
3				
4				

What situations are you facing now in a virtual world that require the use of conflict management skills?

Working in a Virtual World
Summary of Opportunities, Challenges and Strategies

Opportunities	Challenges	Strategies
Participation	• How to build a virtual community. • How to get people to participate fully in an electronic environment independent of their comfort level in groups. • How to identify and assemble the team.	• Provide personal freedom through anywhere/anytime technology. • Develop guidelines for participation. • Rotate meeting sites. • Interact in social ways.
Problem Solving	• How to get partici-pation from the right people with the right skills. • How to get the right person to look at questions. • How to work together across time zones.	• Ensure that everyone is using the same tools. • Encourage resource sharing. • Make a list of priorities. • Allow for 7 × 24 work.
Rewards & Recognition	• How to recognize quiet contributors.	• Reward desired behaviors and actual competence vs. perception of competence.
Learning	• How to facilitate group learning.	• Capture and document ideas. • Assign someone to actively facilitate the Team Room. • Create mechanisms for building collective intelligence.

(Working in a Virtual World continues on next page)

Working in a Virtual World *(concluded)*

Opportunities	Challenges	Strategies
Personal Opportunities	• How to share knowledge and skills.	• Hold world-wide meetings at different locations.
Communications	• How to communicate effectively in the absence of traditional cues. • How to interpret tone. • How to interpret "no response" to questions. • How to relate to team members who have English as a second language. • How to relate with people who are not comfortable communicating in writing.	• Build in opportunities for face-to-face communications. • Set norms regarding communication. • Put pictures with names wherever possible; use visuals. • Use short, to-the-point sentences. • Whether or not there are face-to-face meetings, listen and demonstrate understanding.
Trust	• How to balance task orientation vs. people orientation. • How to minimize invasiveness. • How to reduce the threat associated with information sharing. • How to maintain a base of understanding.	• Develop norms around cultural differences. • Strive for equity of time convenience. • Avoid magnifying and personalizing off-hand comments.

**YOUR
TURN**

Which of the challenges and strategies presented in the chart on pages 108 and 109 is most relevant to your situation?

SKILL 7:
DEMONSTRATE LEADERSHIP

- **Definition:** Walking the talk
- **Benefits:**
    - Elevates others to a leadership role
    - Role models desired behaviors
- **Steps:**
    A. Lead virtually
    B. Facilitate teamwork
    C. Manage team communications

Introduction
With all the books on leadership in the last decade, the role of team leader has now taken on extraordinary expectations.

Organizations today now expect their leaders to:

- Clarify purpose and goals
- Build commitment and self-confidence
- Strengthen collective skills
- Remove obstacles to performance
- Create opportunities for others
- Do real work themselves
- Strike a balance between delegation and doing
- Avoid any action that may intimidate anyone on the team
- Check their ego at the door
- Keep a positive attitude
- Make tough decisions
- Involve the team in decision making
- Guide, but don't control

- Understand what the team needs and what it does not need from the leader
- Listen carefully to understand performance challenges
- Communicate and motivate
- Evaluate talent and performance
- Act as a role model
- Make wise and courageous judgments in the midst of chaos
- Believe in their purpose and their people
- Keep the purpose relevant and meaningful
- Encourage people to take risks for growth and development
- Continuously challenge team members
- Manage relationships both internally and externally
- Advocate effectively for the team
- Avoid blame placing
- Create a "no-excuse-for-poor-performance" environment

With all these expectations, it is no wonder that organizations are sometimes disappointed in the performance of their leaders. While all of these behaviors are important, it is unrealistic to expect all team leaders to possess all the attributes.

Developing our leadership skill focuses on what we believe are three critical steps that account for the large variance in effective leadership:

Step A. Lead virtually
Step B. Facilitate teamwork
Step C. Manage team communications

The *V*irtual Challenge

As if the list of expectations is not long enough, now leaders are expected to be fluent users of new technology and lead by example. They're expected to meet these expectations within an environment that is more diverse and rapidly changing, in which they:

- can't see people
- can't use familiar ways to communicate, and
- can't have the luxury of single-line staff reporting.

Technology creates a new hierarchy within the organization. Those who are comfortable with, are proficient in and promote the use of technology may gain informal status within the organization, regardless of job status.

Technology can create a need for collaboration between persons who might never have interacted with one another before. For instance, the CEO may now need to collaborate with an entry-level, techno-savvy clerk to actualize a vision that will help the whole organization. The traditional job hierarchy and socioeconomic hierarchy may be turned upside down by the technological hierarchy. A leader can gain trust by admitting they need assistance with the technology.

The Weight of Leadership

Be clear
Be committed
Delegate
Decide
Support
Be positive
Involve
Listen
Be courageous
Evaluate
Challenge
Advocate

Step A.
Lead virtually

- **What it means:**
  - Leading teams made up of diverse people in diverse locations
- **How it works:**
  - Develop new skills to relate cross-culturally, think systemically, plan globally
  - Be flexible, open-minded, resilient, and patient
  - Be open to new structures of leadership
  - Have a broad base of knowledge

The Idea

Communicating in a virtual environment requires a unique set of skills and attitudes. In traditional organizations the leader served as the hub for all communications, coordination, and documentation. After downsizing, delayering, and restructuring, however, virtual leaders find themselves acting as facilitators of teams, tasks, and technologies in diverse and distant groups.

In the global economy, surviving managers discover that the old rules no longer apply. Building, leading, and communicating with global teams represent entirely new challenges for today's leader.

Effective virtual leaders are distinguished by their personality, skills, and knowledge. The ideal personality profile of a virtual leader is a person who is:

- Open-minded,
- Creative,
- Resilient,
- Patient,
- Persistent, and
- Adaptive.

Required skills for this job include the ability to relate cross-culturally, think systemically, and plan globally. In addition, successful virtual leaders have a strong base of knowledge in history, anthropology, social psychology and the use of technology. This personality, skill and knowledge profile will contribute significantly to competent communications in the 21st-century team.

While there is a preferred profile, there is no prescribed formula for successful communication in the global economy. Virtual leaders must find their own way through the maze of different rules, values, assumptions, languages, time zones and technologies. There are common themes and tested strategies, however, that have contributed to virtual trust and virtual collaboration on high performing, virtual teams.

Profile of a Virtual Leader

Personality	Skills	Knowledge
Open-minded	Relate cross-culturally	History
Persistent	Think systemically	Social psychology
Adaptive	Plan globally	Anthropology
Resilient		
Creative		
Patient		

**YOUR
TURN**

Using the profile of a virtual leader in the table above, how would you assess your own strengths and weaknesses as a virtual leader?

Step B.
Facilitate teamwork

- **What it means:**
  - Making sure for every business goal the right people with the right skills are participating in positive ways
- **How it works:**
  - Request information
  - Involve others in decisions
  - Credit contributions

The Idea

Teamwork does not just happen, it needs to be facilitated. Leaders encourage teamwork in several ways. They:

- Establish a positive climate;
- Promote participation;
- Empower the team;
- Model teamwork with peers; and
- Reinforce established team behaviors.

For leaders to establish a positive climate they need to:

- Provide ongoing opportunities for team members to share their thoughts and feelings,
- Pay attention to personal needs,
- Treat each person as a unique individual,
- Show respect,
- Look for what is right in each team member's ideas and actions,
- Show interest non-verbally,
- Promote each person,
- Use language team members understand.

Leaders can encourage participation by getting team members involved in various activities. Three techniques are particularly useful:

- **Requesting information**—asking team members to talk about a particular topic. In a virtual environment, where leaders may not be able to see non-verbal cues, it is even more important to hear the verbal cues.

- **Involving others in decisions**—including the right people, the right organizations and the right geographies. This step is especially important on a virtual team because the familiar pattern is to involve only the people who are physically available.

- **Crediting**—recognizing and acknowledging individual contributions to the team. Recognizing contributions requires that the leader identify what team members are saying and doing that are adding value to the team. Crediting in a virtual environment means making the invisible visible, i.e., making remote members' presence felt.

The leader must also have insight about individual contributions to the team. The scale below is a way of assessing the individuals in the group according to participation level:

Type of participant	Level of involvement
Leader	Assumes responsibility for team progress
Contributor	Assumes responsibility for own learning and progress—does more than expected
Participant	Meets expectations
Observer	Does not actually participate with the team—does less than what is expected
Detractor	Gets in the way of progress

Effective leaders not only assess where team members are on this scale, but also look for ways to help each member move up on the scale. It is easy to write people off when there are difficulties, particularly when they are far away. Good leaders resist the temptation of blaming the other person for the difficulty.

Virtual leaders recognize that different people have different skills and corresponding comfort levels communicating by writing, speaking or using technology. Effective leaders notice who is participating in what forms of communication, and they make accurate judgments about who is just "showing off" and who is actually contributing.

Example
The Team Leader observed that Jim changed from being a contributor in small group discussions to being only an observer when discussion involved the entire team. The leader asked Jim about this and learned that Jim felt overwhelmed in the larger group and believed his contribution was less important than some of the star players of the group. The leader took the opportunity during the next large group meeting to publicly credit Jim's participation and importance within the group. The group started noticing Jim's contributions appearing in electronic databases and gave him positive feedback. Crediting Jim's abilities within the group gave Jim the confidence to participate in larger group discussions.

The Virtual Challenge

Facilitating teamwork in a virtual environment is particularly challenging because people in different locations don't have the opportunity to bond outside the team environment. Leaders need to develop skills and sensitivities to facilitate remote communication among team members from multiple functions, organizations and cultures.

In addition, facilitating teamwork may require leaders to stretch themselves and take risks, learn new skills and reach out to other team members in a new way.

**YOUR
TURN**

*What are the most frequently used options for
communicating in your group?*

☐ *Face-to-face meetings?* ☐ *E-Mail?*

☐ *Discussion databases?* ☐ *Voice mail?*

☐ *Video conferencing?* ☐ *Telephone?* ☐ *Others?*

Are these options used appropriately?

*How do the communication norms need to change to
improve every option?*

*Are good discriminations made about when to use which
option?*

*In regard to team communications, what does your team
pay the most attention to: content, process or context?
What does your team pay the least attention to? How
could each of these elements be improved?*

Step C.
Manage team communications

- **What it means:**
  - — Improving the effectiveness of time spent together
  - — Improving focus
- **How it works:**
  - — Prepare before meetings and post meeting time, agenda and participants
  - — Set the purpose, agenda and limits during the meeting
  - — Follow up on action commitments after the meeting
  - — Use workgroup technology to communicate action links to other teams or individuals

The Idea

Most teams spend a great deal of time in meetings. In traditional teams, meetings are the most frequent way to check in with team members to ensure that everyone is on track and not at cross purposes. Meetings also provide an opportunity to share information, gain support, reconnect with the mission and promote team unity. However, in a virtual team, meetings may take on a secondary role in team communications. Leaders need to find additional ways to facilitate team check-in, updates and team unity.

When meetings are the appropriate context for team communication, leaders can do a great deal to improve the effectiveness of the meeting.

Before the meeting, a leader can post an agenda and let participants know how they can best prepare for the meeting. Distributing materials relevant to the meeting can be an effective way to get everyone on the "same page" before the meeting starts.

Also, a leader can seek input from team members on the meeting agenda so that they feel involved. The Team Facilitator can post the meeting time, participants and agenda items. Team members can add their comments to the agenda or add items. In this way, all members involved in the meeting can be informed about additions to the agenda and know all the players before they get to the meeting.

In a physical meeting, team members can see who else is attending the meeting. In a virtual meeting, it is necessary to inform everyone of who is participating in the meeting.

In some cases, a facilitator may be assigned so that the meeting can run smoothly and the leader can be free to focus on the content and context without having to worry about "running the meeting."

The meeting facilitator:

- Keeps the meeting from drifting off on irrelevant topics;
- Keeps things moving by asking for consensus when appropriate; and
- Summarizes solutions.

The leader also ensures that action commitments are summarized at the end of the meeting so that each person knows what they are responsible for.

The leader should include the following actions when running a meeting:

- State the purpose, agenda and limits for the meeting;
- Indicate which items are for information sharing;
- Indicate which items are for problem solving;
- Summarize action commitments at the end.

After the meeting, the leader can follow up on the action commitments to ensure that progress is being made and to see if any team members require support or further direction. The leader can also ask for critiques of the meeting and for suggestions for improvement.

The Team Recorder takes notes during the meeting and posts the notes on the electronic database afterward.

The Virtual Challenge

While meetings constitute the primary means of communication in a traditional team, there are multiple options for communicating on a technology-enabled, virtual team. Virtual leaders need to think about the desired outcome for every type of communication and then decide on the appropriate process. For example, a performance evaluation should be a one-on-one, face-to-face communication, but information sharing to the group can easily be conducted in an electronic space. Unfortunately, valuable face-to-face time is often wasted by presenting data that could be shared more efficiently by other means. Leaders who communicate effectively give thoughtful consideration to the content, process and context of all vital communication.

Decisions about communication process and context may change as the team progresses through the Seven Stages of Development discussed in the introduction to the first task. Particularly in the Renewal Stage, virtual leaders need to reconsider all elements of communication. The content may focus on learnings from successes and failures. The process may consist of brainstorming techniques that can be facilitated electronically or face-to-face.

And, most importantly the leader needs to create an environment, or context, in which people feel free to express both positive and negative thoughts and feelings so that the team can generate new learnings that can be applied to the next "spike" in the "fishnet."

(The Virtual Challenge is continued on next page)

124

The Virtual Challenge *(concluded)*

Meetings can be an effective way to further progress on virtual teams because so much of the work is done in isolation. Workgroup technology can be used to post meeting times, allow team members to respond to the agenda, post meeting minutes and link information to additional team members affected by the decisions made during the meeting.

Team members should come prepared to meetings. The challenge is to bring resources that will help you express yourself in a virtual environment. Prepare notes that are readily faxable and have files available. Leverage the technology to your advantage. For example, if you prepare graphics, charts or displays ahead of time, you can use the technology to allow all team members to view or even manipulate the information at the same time.

Having real time meetings on-line can pose special challenges to team members and require new sets of skills. On-line meetings strip away the rich subtext of information we receive from body language and verbal cues (e.g., raised eyebrow, deep sigh, smirk or nod of approval). Participating in on-line meetings requires more risk-taking and more thoughtful presentation of ideas. Having to compose ideas in writing may take more time for some, making it difficult for them to jump into fast-paced discussion. Even a lack of typing skills can create barriers to participation.

It is important for team leaders to monitor individual participation and help team members overcome their resistance.

YOUR
TURN

Use the space below to write down what you can do to manage communications more effectively.

In the work your team does, what really needs to be communicated face-to-face?

How can we use these skills in a virtual environment? How do we re-define meeting rituals so they are appropriate in the virtual team environment?

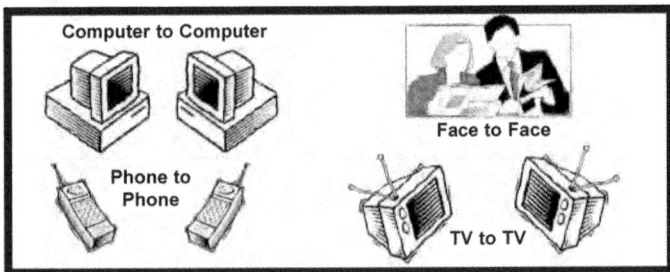

Computer to Computer

Phone to Phone

Face to Face

TV to TV

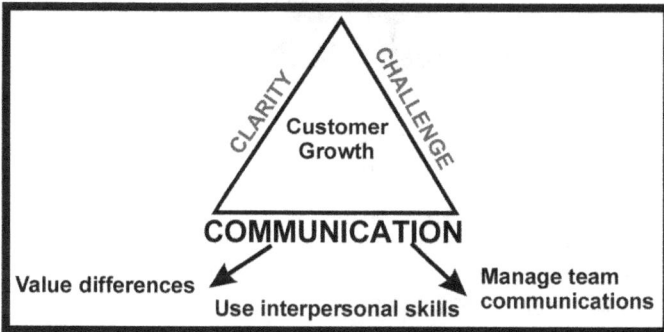

CLARITY / CHALLENGE

Customer
Growth

COMMUNICATION

Value differences ← Use interpersonal skills → Manage team communications

Task III. Communication Exercise

In this task you learned three skills:

• Value differences
• Use interpersonal skills
• Manage team communications

Please review the three skills and decide what actions you can take in your team to improve communications.

Task III. Summary

Communication and conflict resolution are a priority for working smoothly in groups, particularly groups working together in a virtual environment.

On teams today, there is a diversity of personalities, capabilities and even national cultures to deal with. Leveraging this diversity to the advantage of the team means using our strengths and overcoming our weaknesses.

An important part of teamwork involves interpersonal skills including active listening, understanding another's point of view and communicating your view. You learned that working in a virtual environment requires a new set of skills to listen, understand and communicate your view.

In every group situation, conflict is a natural process. Managing conflict by identifying values, exploring alternatives and searching for the best solution goes a long way to developing well-oiled teams.

You learned about leadership and how to facilitate teamwork and manage effective communications. Successful leaders are able to balance workgroup technologies, communication options and individual capabilities with team needs to make the difference between teams that work together in conflict and missed assignments and teams that work together in trust and collaboration.

SUMMARY

> • Prioritize major issues and opportunities
> • Develop common purpose and principles
> • Establish a plan
> • Define roles and responsibilities
> • Value differences
> • Use interpersonal skills
> • Demonstrate leadership

In this team development book you have learned a variety of skills to establish a strong foundation for your team.

You also gained methods for working within the virtual team environment. At the beginning of any team project it is important to lay the groundwork that all members of the team feel a part of and agree to. You did this by identifying challenges and opportunities, determining the important issues and setting problem-solving priorities.

To develop a common purpose you created a vision statement, defined the values for your team and agreed on a set of norms that your team would operate within.

By establishing a plan you created a framework and attitude that sets the tone for the work to be done. Defining the mission and establishing goals allowed each team member to have a clear definition of where the team is going.

The next step was to define how you were going to get there. Assigning roles, responsibilities and the tasks to be done provided more specific direction to team members individually. At this time the project schedule was created by determining the key events and milestones and analyzing how they fit together interdependently.

Once the foundation was formed, it was time to get down to implement the tasks. Interpersonal skills and conflict resolution were essential for working smoothly within the group. In this book you learned important skills for valuing differences, listening and understanding as well as communicating your view. In every group situation, conflict is a natural process. Managing conflict by identifying values, exploring alternatives and searching for the best solution went a long way to developing a well-oiled work team.

Finally, you learned about leadership and how to facilitate teamwork and manage effective communications.

Throughout this book, you also gained insight into how workgroup technology assists in the process of team development in a virtual environment and how working virtually creates new challenges and opportunities.

High performing teams give their company a competitive edge by being flexible, more productive, more market responsive and more diverse. Whether your team is working in the same place at the same time or working any place at any time, these techniques for developing teamwork will increase the likelihood that your team will become a high performance team.

Being a member of a high performing team can be extremely rewarding both professionally and personally. We hope that you can walk away from this book with new skills to ensure that your team becomes a high performing team.

Bibliography

Bancroft, Nancy H. *New Partnerships for Managing Technological Change.* New York: John Wiley & Sons, Inc., 1992.

Bass, Bernard M. and Avolio, Bruce J. "Transformational Leadership and Organizational Culture." *Public Administration Quarterly,* Spring 1993; Vol. 17; No. 1; Pp. 30–41.

Bolton, Robert. *People Skills.* New York: Simon & Schuster, Inc., 1979.

Brooks, Ann Marie T. *Team Building.* Baltimore, MD: Williams & Wilkins, 1990.

Buchholz, Steve. *Creating the High-Performance Team.* New York: John Wiley & Sons, Inc., 1987.

Carkhuff, Robert R. *The Art of Helping VIII.* Amherst, MA: Human Resource Development Press, 2000.

Carkhuff, Robert R. *The Age of the New Capitalism.* Amherst, MA: Human Resource Development Press, 1993.

Carkhuff, Robert R. *Toward Actualizing Human Potential.* Amherst, MA: Human Resource Development Press, 1981.

Carkhuff, Robert R. and Berenson, Bernard. *Beyond Counseling and Therapy.* New York: Holt, Rinehart, Winston, 1967.

Dunphy, Dexter and Stace, Doug. "The Strategic Management of Corporate Change." *Human Relations,* August 1993; Vol. 46; No. 8; Pg. 905.

Dyer, William C. *Team Building: Current Issues and New Alternatives.* Reading, MA: Addison-Wesley, 1995.

Fiorelli, Joseph and Feller, Richard. "Re-engineering TQM and Work Redesign: An Integrative Approach to Continuous Organizational Excellence." *Public Administration Quarterly,* Spring 1994; Vol. 15; No. 1; Pp. 54–63.

Francis, Dave. *Improving Work Groups: A Practical Manual for Team Building.* San Diego, CA: University Associates, 1979.

Fulmer, Robert M. "A Model for Changing the Way Organizations Learn: Learning Organizations Build Knowledge Bridges." *Planning Review,* May 1994; Vol. 22; No. 3; Pg. 20.

Goldman, Steven L. *Agile Competitors and Virtual Organizations: Strategies for Enriching the Customer.* New York: Van Nostrand Reinhold, 1995.

Harrington-Mackin, Deborah. *The Team Building Tool Kit: Tips, Tactics and Rules for Effective Workplace Teams.* New York: New Directions Management Services, Inc., 1994.

Johansen, Robert. *Leading Business Teams.* Reading, MA: Addison-Wesley, 1991.

Johnson, Sam T. "Work Teams: What's Ahead in Work Design and Rewards Management." *Compensation and Benefits Review,* March 1993, Vol. 25; No. 2; Pg. 35.

Ju, Yanan and Cushman, Donald P. *Organizational Teamwork In High-Speed Management.* Albany, NY: State University of New York Press, 1995.

Kanungo, Rabindra N. and Conger, Jay A. "Promoting Altruism as a Corporate Goal." *Executive,* August 1993; Vol. 7; No. 3; Pp. 37–48.

Knight, Fred S. "Organizational Development Shouldn't Mean Organizational Devastation." *Business Communications Review,* November 1993; Vol. 23; No. 11; Pg. 6; Editorial.

Lorenz, Christopher. "A New Mindset for the Manager—Christopher Lorenz Reports on the Obstacles to Change." *Financial Times,* February 16, 1994, Wednesday; Management; Pg. 19.

McClelland, Sam. "Gaining Competitive Advantage Through Strategic Management Development (SMD)." *Journal of Management Development,* 1994; Vol. 13; No. 5; Pp. 4–13.

McLeod, Poppy Lauretta. "Are Human-Factors People Really So Different? Comparisons of Interpersonal Behavior and Implications for Design Teams." *Journal of Management Information Systems,* Summer 1992; Vol. 9; No. 1; Pp. 113–132.

Maznevski, Martha L. "Understanding Our Differences: Performance in Decision-Making Groups With Diverse Members." *Human Relations,* May 1994; Vol. 47; No. 5; Pg. 531.

Marson, Brian. "Building Customer-Focused Organizations in British Columbia." *Public Administration Quarterly,* Spring 1993, Vol. 17; No. 1; Pp. 112–121.

Moxton, Peter. *Building a Better Team: A Handbook for Managers and Facilitators.* Aldershot: Cower Publishing, 1993.

Nevis, Edwin C., DiBella, Anthony J., Could, Janet M. "Understanding Organizations as Learning Systems." *Sloan Management Review,* January 1995; Vol. 36; No. 2; Pg. 73.

Olson, Margrethe H. *Technological Support for Work Group Collaboration.* Hillsdale, NJ: Lawrence Erlbaum Associates, Inc., 1989.

Opper, Susanna and Ferkso-Weiss, Henry. *Technology for Teams: Enhancing Productivity in Networked Organizations.* New York: Van Nostrand Reinhold, 1992.

Osborne, Richard L. "Entrepreneurial Renewal: Preventing Professional Burnout." *Business Horizons,* November 1992; Vol. 35; No. 6; Pg. 58.

Pascale, Richard. "The Benefit of a Clash of Opinions." *Personnel Management,* October 1993; Vol. 25; No. 10; Pg. 38; Includes related article.

Portis, Bernard. "Making Canadian Employee Involvement a Quality Effort." *Journal for Quality & Participation,* October/November 1994; Vol. 17; No. 6; Pp. 24–27.

PR Newswire, January 12, 1995, Thursday, *Financial News.* "What Makes Manufacturing Teamwork Veterans Tick?" Survey Results Highlight Varied Rewards. Woodstock, IL, January 12.

Reddy, W. Brendan. *Team Building.* Alexandria, VA: NTL Institute for Applied Behavioral Science, 1988.

Reger, Rhonda K., Gustafson, Loren T., Demarie, Samuel N., Mullane, John V. "Reframing the Organization: Why Implementing Total Quality is Easier Said Than Done." *Academy of Management Review,* July 1994; Vol. 19; No. 3; Pg. 565.

Schrage, Michael. *No More Teams!* New York: Currency Doubleday, 1995.

Spitzer, T. Quinn and Tregoe, Benjamin. "Thinking and Managing Beyond the Boundaries: Management in a Globalized Business Environment." *Business Horizons,* January 1993; Vol. 36; No. 1; Pg. 36.

Strauss, Norman. "Make Your Visions Valid and Viable." *Management Today,* February 1993; Pg. 92.

Weisbord, Marvin R. *Productive Workplaces.* San Francisco: Jossey-Bass, 1987.

White, Louis P. and Rhodeback, Melanie J. "Ethical Dilemmas in Organization Development: A Cross-Cultural Analysis." *Journal of Business Ethics,* September 1992; Vol. 11; No. 9; Pp. 663–670.

Wills, Gordon. "Your Enterprise School of Management: Actionable Learning." *Journal of Management Development,* 1993. Vol. 12; No. 2; Pp. 36–41.

Woodcock, Mike. *Team Development Manual.* New York: Wiley, 1979.

Index

www.ingramcontent.com/pod-product-compliance
Lightning Source LLC
Chambersburg PA
CBHW031123210326
41519CB00047B/4499